Influencing Enterprise Risk Mitigation

Influencing Enterprise Risk Mitigation

Second Edition

Francis J. D'Addario

AMSTERDAM · BOSTON · HEIDELBERG · LONDON
NEW YORK · OXFORD · PARIS · SAN DIEGO
SAN FRANCISCO · SINGAPORE · SYDNEY · TOKYO

Security
Executive Council

Elsevier
The Boulevard, Langford Lane, Kidlington, Oxford, OX5 1GB, UK
225 Wyman Street, Waltham, MA 02451, USA

Originally published by the Security Executive Council, 2009

Notices
Knowledge and best practice in this field are constantly changing. As new research and
experience broaden our understanding, changes in research methods, professional practices,
or medical treatment may become necessary.

Practitioners and researchers must always rely on their own experience and knowledge in
evaluating and using any information, methods, compounds, or experiments described
herein. In using such information or methods they should be mindful of their own safety
and the safety of others, including parties for whom they have a professional responsibility.

To the fullest extent of the law, neither the Publisher nor the authors, contributors, or
editors, assume any liability for any injury and/or damage to persons or property as a
matter of products liability, negligence or otherwise, or from any use or operation of any
methods, products, instructions, or ideas contained in the material herein.

British Library Cataloguing-in-Publication Data
A catalogue record for this book is available from the British Library

Library of Congress Cataloging-in-Publication Data
A catalog record for this book is available from the Library of Congress

ISBN: 978-0-12-417233-3

For more publications in the Elsevier Risk Management and Security
Collection, visit our website at store.elsevier.com/SecurityExecutiveCouncil.

This book has been manufactured using Print On Demand technology. Each copy is
produced to order and is limited to black ink. The online version of this book will show
color figures where appropriate.

Working together
to grow libraries in
developing countries

www.elsevier.com • www.bookaid.org

Printed and bound by CPI Group (UK) Ltd, Croydon, CR0 4YY
Transferred to digital print 2013

DEDICATION

This is dedicated in loving memory of Aaron David Goodrich, Emory Allen Evans, and Mary Caitrin Mahoney, who were tragically murdered by Carl Cooper in a Washington, DC, Starbucks on the July 4th weekend of 1997; and to Tony McNaughton, who stepped into harm's way to save his employee in Vancouver, BC, in 2000. All victims inspire us to continuous protection improvement. With their survivors we pray that no risk goes unlearned to inform a safer and more secure future.

CONTENTS

ACKNOWLEDGMENTS

The art and science of persuasive security influence requires sharing both our successes and shortcomings. Security subject matter can be sensitive. Counterintuitively, we tend to hide our knowledge in hopes that our secrets will keep us safe, rather than sharing it with our neighbors to create more secure communities. Enabling others to create thoughtful cultures of care often requires revisiting events that might sooner be comfortably forgotten. Situations and dilemmas that continue to threaten us must be addressed or we are doomed to be re-victimized by preventable and mitigatable hazards. Innovation requires both data leadership and courage. Many thanks are owed to those who have had the courage to help me and my teams protect others.

I was greatly influenced by the vision of Howard Schultz and a cadre of diversely talented individuals. When I was a boy my mother warranted that if she ever came into money she would be inclined to "spread it around." Howard did that and more, simply by sharing opportunities for several hundred thousand talented Starbucks partners, thousands of dedicated farmers, and millions of loyal customers. Howard did not do it alone. He adopted a community that in turn adopted him.

I owe thanks to a number of other leaders including Howard Behar, Orin Smith, Dave Olsen, Michael Casey, Howard Wollner, Rick Arthur, Bruce Craig, Gregg Johnson, Jim Alling, Troy Alstead, Cliff Burrows, Dorothy Kim, Dub Hay, and Ted Garcia. I am forever indebted to the Partner and Asset Protection team who breathed life into the mantra: "Protect people. Secure assets. Contribute margin. Enable mission." To name a few, Phil Hummel, who promised Starbucks "cared as much about its people as its product;" Ken Kelly, who brought experience with empathy; Nick Mainardi, with his eye for talent and a means for developing it; as well as Rick Gipson, who attended many of the unsung details of implementation. Each developed protection professionals and protocols to meld security accountability with the benefit of the doubt.

I am grateful to an innovative supporting cast and contributing team managers including Barb Padagas, Sean Dettloff, and Marc Osborn, who effectively tackled new challenges along with Ed Amdahl, Kimberly Hughes, Lee Ann Dickson, Mike Haucke, Molly Nollette, and Steve Powers. Their teams answered the bell around the clock, expanding a protection umbrella across the globe with the capable assistance of Cecilia DeFranco, Dean Correia, Joe Nekic, Greg Brumley, Krista Osborne, Mark Zivilik, Peter Wood, Rudy Wang, Sally Kee, and Steven Bova.

I have personally and professionally benefited from the advice of cross-functional subject matter expertise from Audrey Lincoff, Charity Peck, Chris Schultz, Deb Vasseur, Denise Bakken, Elizabeth King, Jen O'Connor, Jerry Vergeront, Jim Bennett, Jim Morgan, Jon Engle, Karen Metro, Kelly Hall, Kevin Stock, Khoi Tran, Linda Trautman, Lucy Helm, Matt Swaya, Megan Lantz, Norm Oulette, Norma Miller, Pam Harkins, Paula Boggs, Peter Torrebiarte, Rich Soderberg, Robert Vu, Ross Anderson, Sid Javheri, Steve Legg, Steve Prosser, Sue Mecklenburg, Val O'Neil, and their associates.

Security service provider expertise also influenced my worldview, including those rendered by collaborators at ASI, CAP Index, Control Risks, Crime Prevention Associates, Diebold, GE, ISO, OSAC, PACOM, SAIC, SOS, Travelers, etc. In particular, I appreciated the efforts of Ben Casterline, Bob Hayes, David Lattin, Ewan McPhie, Isac Tabib, Pat Gerstle, Pete Rampp, Randy Koch, Steve O'Malley, and their colleagues. I hold their informed opinion, assistance, and that of their confederates in high regard. My professional peer influences range from members of ASIS, ACFE, and ISMA to the Security Executive Council. Thanks to all who contributed and apologies to those not explicitly listed.

I also owe all those who shared their talent in my formative years including Pete Shaulis, Don Sperling, Billie Taylor, Rose Narva, Bill Letsky, Hal Graves, Bob Buhrig, Dick Nelson, Ray Johnson, Warren Rosenthal, Ernie Renaud, Richard Pitcock, Deborah Hollis, Mike Arrighi, Vince Cowdry, and Fran Tesorero. They served their clients well in Baltimore and the reaches of Sears, Southland, Jerrico, and Hardees.

I am indebted to my prepublication readers for their keen eyes and welcome observations including: Jack Blevins, Bruce Blythe, Brad Brekke, Pamela Collins, Dean Correia, Mike Howard, Laura Laughlin, Lew McCreary, Dennis Moriarty, Les Nichols, Norm Saunders, and John Smith.

Finally, and most appreciatively, I am grateful for the considerable efforts and insights of my editors including my life partner Louise D'Addario of Crime Prevention Associates and Kathleen Kotwica, Chief Knowledge Strategist of the Security Executive Council, without whose efforts this book would not be possible. Special kudos are due to my children, extended family, and friends who listened patiently, suffered silently, and offered me the benefit of the doubt.

FOREWORD

INTERDEPENDENT COMMUNITIES REQUIRE PROTECTION

The seeds of this book flew like the wind with the TGV train from Paris to Dijon in 2004. I hoped they might take root at our destination, a 14th century chateau in the French countryside. Dijon, the historic provincial capital of Burgundy, was the site of a Starbucks Coffee and Tea Buyers Summit hosted by Dub Hay, senior vice president of Coffee and Procurement. Our primary objective was to influence a group of intrepid world travelers to consider the merits of hazards intelligence and precautionary travel security. My role was enterprise risk mitigation in my capacity as chief security strategist.

Coffee and tea buyers are a relatively independent lot who have historically relied on their own wits to tramp the beautiful yet risky destinations of Africa, Asia, Central America, South America, and islands of the Pacific. Starbucks Arabica coffee grows at elevations around 5,000 feet, typically between the Tropics of Cancer and Capricorn. Tea and botanicals also thrive there at lower elevations. Moderate- to high-risk origins include Colombia, Ethiopia, Guatemala, India, Indonesia, Kenya, Rwanda, Papua New Guinea, Sri Lanka, Tanzania, and their neighbors.

Those who trek the path to coffee and tea country experience the palpable hazards of unimproved roads, poorly equipped transportation, security forces with dubious intent, and scarce resources to mitigate mishaps. Revolutionary and government agents personified by teenagers with automatic weapons may require nominal tribute before allowing passage beyond hastily contrived toll barriers. Police stations may feature hand grenade netting and the telltale scars of past gun battles. In contrast, Dijon did not require one eye on the road ahead and another behind.

David Lattin, my co-presenter and Director of Specialty Insurance for Travelers, and I both knew there was an uphill climb as influencers. Most of the audience had a hundred thousand miles or more of high-risk travel under their belts without catastrophic incident. We knew from experience that intelligently communicated risk mitigation would enhance trip safety. Our opportunity was to urge adoption of sustainable security practices.

I first met David at his previous employ instructing a Control Risks crisis management workshop. His years as a naval intelligence and peace officer had served him well. David's impressive history expedited secure solutions for the stickiest risk dilemmas. I also knew that one summit attendee, Peter Torrebiarte, director of Farmer Support, had benefited from training he had received. Prior to Starbucks, Peter was kidnapped in Guatemala and held in peril for weeks prior to a successful repatriation to his family. Peter had agreed to share aspects of his ordeal to support our effort.

Our reception in Dijon warmed with introductions and small talk. The usual exchange of personal history and employment tends to shrink the globe to common denominators. To our surprise Peter and David surmised that David had been the case officer who supervised his release years earlier. They had never met. Rich dialogue ensued in the following days that proved invaluable in forming the elements of the plan to protect people and supply chain. Peter's story personified the risk and mitigation lessons of the agenda. The buyers' anecdotes revealed many tales of "near miss" injury and loss to reinforce the data. They grasped the opportunity to improve the management of their own security and safety.

The health and safety of coffee and tea buyers are strategically essential to Starbucks. These clients arguably represented the finest palates, agronomy, and logistics talent in the world. Contemplated growth, from 4 percent to 44 percent use of the world's highest quality Arabica coffee in five years, was dependent on their health. Buyers are emissaries to the farmers for Coffee and Farmer Equity (C.A.F.E.) practices. They provide resources to incrementally improve the agronomy, crop quality, and community with transparent premium pricing tied to performance objectives. Consumer confidence for five million customer transactions per week depends on the safe transport of buyers and products around the globe. The benefits of security investment play up and down the supply chain from the farmer to the cooperative, roaster, distributor, and retailer. World-class beverage quality is both the end and means to enable protection. It affords livelihoods for several hundred thousand stakeholders.

We acknowledged that we all are students of the world. A global approach was adopted for testing risk awareness, hazard reporting, and medical and security assistance. Collective experience and intelligence eliminated many hazards. Resource adoption enabled risk mitigation improvement with informed behaviors. Travel risk communications, transportation diligence, and itinerary status reporting allowed necessary mitigation of known hazards and provided "just-in-time" response coordinates for emergencies. Often altering a minor leg of a trip involving a significant risk could eliminate a security concern, such as avoiding travel through a major city during a hotly contested election.

At Starbucks the duty to reasonably protect people is nonnegotiable. The mission to be "the premier purveyor of the finest coffee in the world while maintaining uncompromising principles as we grow" depends on the ability to provide a great work environment.[1] That expansive commitment includes safety and security. Monitoring intelligence, agendas, and transportation to provide global support for security and medical emergencies goes far in allaying personal and family anxieties. It also importantly bridges the needs of the farm community to enable premium trade. Supply chain may serve as a metaphor of community codependency.

In the following pages we will explore many of the security and health hazards facing our interdependent global communities. They range from contagion, climate change, and crime to environmental, geological, and geopolitical disasters. Although risk elimination is unlikely, we can influence our outcomes with reasonable resource allocation. Awareness, preparedness, and mitigation are within reach with calculable return on investment. That persuasive case may be made one person and one community at a time. There is not a moment to lose—our safety, security, and sustainability depend on it.

---

[1]Howard Schultz and Dori Jones Yang, *Pour Your Heart Into It* (New York: Hyperion, 1997).

WHAT'S PAST IS PROLOGUE

Few hazards will surprise the student of risk mitigation. Historical data informs. Both natural and manmade catastrophes will occur with varying certainty over time. Our opportunity is influencing outcomes with awareness, preparedness, and good mitigation practices.

William Shakespeare acutely observed that our past is predictive of the future.[1] The past certainly informs most protection practitioners and their approach to security risk and mitigation. It did mine prior to my interview for the global security leadership position at Starbucks Coffee in May of 1997.

Consequential risks were not new to me, nor were measurable security risk mitigations. My previous security teams had managed the aftermath of more than 60 workplace homicides, hundreds of injuries, and countless threats to people and assets costing untold anguish and millions of dollars. Importantly, my teams had innovated, tested, implemented, and measured effective security practices for significant risk reduction and return on investment.

Data and experience formed my view that commercial armed robbery posed a primary risk to all cash-handling businesses. In responding to an interview question regarding priorities, I mentioned that Starbucks was no exception to this hazard. I was a bit taken aback when my interviewers expressed uncertainty. It was apparent that my assessment of this potential impediment to Starbucks global aspirations was more or less received as a personal opinion.

This high-growth organization was learning its way, like a talented adolescent eager to travel but inexperienced in the risks that lay ahead. Interview panels followed with questions and comments that illustrated diverse concerns for other looming hazards, including risks to assets: cash, inventory, information, manufacturing and supply

---

[1] *The Tempest*, 2.1.243-44. Reference is to act, scene, and line.

chain. Terrorism and pandemic were remote possibilities in 1997. Armed robbery violence seemed equally unlikely to some.

There was a persuasive case to be made for prioritizing commercial armed robbery risk. Several comprehensive studies and behavioral science applications proofed prior to 1997 resulted in significant incidence and injury risk reductions. I shared the data that had enabled my previous teams to significantly reduce the frequency and severity of violent events at three international corporations while facilitating cost containment, growth, and significant contribution to profit margin.

The armed robbery hazard in North America was well documented by the Western Behavioral Science Institute (WBSI), the National Association of Convenience Stores (NACS), Athena Research, and the National Food Service Security Council (NFSSC). The US National Institute for Occupational Safety and Health (NIOSH) had published extensive guidelines for preventing workplace violence.[2] The convenience and quick service segments had moved decisively to curb the risk. Robbery incidence reductions of more than 50 percent were common. Many companies had mitigated robbery hazards using layered and integrated security approaches featuring crime prevention design, risk awareness training, cash control, and security technology.

There was much more than the numbers I left unsaid—the parade of victims I held close. I remembered their faces from happier times as well as the anguish of family and friends. I remembered their pitiful assailants. I was committed to making the workplace safe enough for my children and was passionately inclined to influence others to that reasonable goal.

Having read the Starbucks mission and guiding principles, I intuitively connected my risk assessment to the company's cultural imperative to provide a great workplace. After the interviews I remained uncertain of my employment chances. I knew from insiders that there was a "culture of consensus" at Starbucks. I had witnessed little consensus but was nevertheless excited to have the opportunity to influence the strategy. Opportunities to protect a rising global brand are few and far between.

---

[2] Jenkins, "Violence in the Workplace."

Although grateful to receive the job offer on July 1, my enthusiasm was checked days later on the July 4 weekend when I deeply regretted learning that three Starbucks partners were found murdered in the manager's office area, next to the safe, in the relatively safe Georgetown section of Washington, DC, in an apparent botched robbery attempt. During the weeks prior to joining the company I advised the cross-functional leadership group that convened to manage the aftermath. From the beginning of my career with Starbucks to this writing, that event has profoundly influenced my careful consideration of the consequences of risk and the benefits of mitigation.

This book contains a number of stories that are intended to help readers improve their own personal security while influencing the protection of their families, communities, and organizations. We will cover a range of hazards from our local neighborhood to the region, country, and globe. We will assess philosophy, methodology, and data to make the case for good security practices that empirically mitigate risk and its attendant anxiety.

Practices capable of return on investment include risk awareness; hazard detection and response; and injury, loss, and cost mitigation. We will never be threat-free. Yet we can afford to effectively recognize risk, reduce hazardous incidents, and mitigate consequences to continuously improve outcomes.

Shortly after my arrival at Starbucks I learned that one of my interviewers claimed I "predicted" the 1997 triple homicide. That was inaccurate. I merely observed that the commercial armed robbery hazard featured both frequency and severity for the industry segment. Surmising the likelihood of injury in a frequent threat environment is like anticipating the eventuality of a drowning in a 100-year flood plain. The severity of a foreseeable unmitigated outcome is nearly certain over time. Only the intervals of occurrence vary.

Data may instruct both hazard probabilities and impact consequences. Charting community or organization event history, benchmarking comparable communities, and assessing risk adjacency including network interconnectivity are recommended. Questions will arise. How likely is a risk? What is the frequency? Will it evolve in the community or chance to travel from other quarters? How severe is the impact?

Hazards are more or less predictable by virtue of their tendency to repeat over time. Risk frequency for all hazards may range from minutes to a year or longer periods of measurement depending on the size, breadth, and niche of the institution. All, including near geologic time, help forecast impacts on people and assets taking climate, cultural demographics, geology, geography, sociopolitical conditions, and historical incidents into account.

Robbery violence is no different. As with other hazards, commitment and resources can mitigate the frequency and severity. The Georgetown murders were a body blow. I was struck by the sense of palpable loss throughout Starbucks—from the baristas to the chairman of the board. I witnessed for the first time in my professional career a company that owned the consequence of tragedy to its core and was compelled not to repeat it.

Following the Starbucks homicides, the existing loss prevention department was renamed Partner and Asset Protection (P&AP). This new identity communicated a service level agreement within the organization. The departmental mission was: "Protect people. Secure assets. Contribute margin." Those were the priorities in order. P&AP was to become an enabler of the global Starbucks experience from remote country origins to manufacturing and stores distributed around the world.

The priority was suppression of commercial armed robbery. Other global risks could wait. The Georgetown homicides had badly shaken security confidence across the enterprise. P&AP pressed forward to improve the chances that this kind of tragedy would not happen again. The mitigation of this risk would boost the investment confidence of stakeholders for addressing other hazards.

Employees at Starbucks are called "partners." Stock ownership and health benefits for part-time employees were unique offerings in the early 1990s. Starbucks enjoyed meteoric success with its people-centric approach. Howard Behar, former chief operating officer, was fond of stipulating: "We are not in the coffee business serving people, we are in the people business serving coffee." That mantra, made famous in his 2007 book, *It's Not About the Coffee*, became a litmus test for performance. Partnerships also extend to other relationships including license and joint venture agreements as well as critical service dependencies.

Starbucks, like other highly ethical companies, strategically chose a path wider than simple business objectives, as is evidenced in its mission statement, an excerpt of which is included below.[3] Community missions for highly respected brands are often underpinned by visionary goals as well as requirements for principled conduct that may evolve to a culture of care.

Our Coffee
It has always been, and will always be, about quality. We're passionate about ethically sourcing the finest coffee beans, roasting them with great care, and improving the lives of people who grow them. We care deeply about all of this; our work is never done.

Since 2007, Ethisphere, an international think tank concerned with business ethics, corporate social responsibility, anticorruption, and sustainability, has compiled a list of the world's most ethical companies. The purpose of the annual list, according to Ethisphere, is to honor those "companies that truly go beyond making statements about doing business 'ethically' and translate those words into action."[4] Starbucks is one of 15 companies that have made the list every year.

My intention is to emphasize that principled conduct includes influencing recognition of risk that can move organization or community stakeholders toward more effective mitigation.

Stakeholders are persons with vested interest, from hourly employees to the board of directors including customers, service providers, investors, volunteers, and their dependents. Community stakeholders may range from village residents to national citizenry including neighbors and distanced trade partners or allies. All may be influenced to address risk for mutually beneficial outcomes of improved safety, security, and prosperity.

Sharing relative success is valuable for organizations, large or small. Good and best practices evolve to protect individuals, family, neighbors, and community. Our safety, livelihood, and aspirations depend on how we acknowledge hazards and manage their consequences. Principled pursuit of mission begets trust. The case can be made that

---

[3]Starbucks Corporation, "Our Starbucks Mission Statement."
[4]Ethisphere, "World's Most Ethical Companies."

security confidence is a primary enabler of mission. Conversely, security anxiety can breed distrust.

Turbulent economic conditions exacerbated by poverty, famine, and water scarcity widen the gap between the haves and the have-nots. Disaster recovery capacity is thin. Financial resources are imperiled or lacking for even routine regional emergencies such as severe weather and seismic events that endanger large populations and assets including the fragile infrastructure and critical processes that we depend on to mitigate or recover from an event. Trust in institutions including governments has eroded.

We will likely witness rising crime and violence in the very near future as employment and resources contract. This book will make the strategic and tactical case for risk mitigation to ensure institutional and community resiliency.

We must be prepared, supplied, equipped, trained, and insured for emergency prevention response and to mitigate consequences if prevention fails. This will require anticipating risk events and prioritizing mitigation investment to improve our chances to survive or avoid unnecessary injury or loss. We may also be required to rise to the occasion self-sufficiently when others, including government emergency services, are not there to help us. All must be involved to incrementally improve our chances for success.

The responsibility for emergency and crisis preparedness is shifting. The private sector is estimated to manage up to 80 percent of our critical infrastructure. The US Department of Homeland Security has identified key risk considerations by critical infrastructure subsectors. Comprehensive risk-based mitigation strategies have been adopted for agriculture and food, banking and finance, chemical, commercial facilities, communications, dams, defense industrial, emergency services, energy, government facilities, information technology, national monuments and icons, nuclear, postal and shipping, public health care, transportation systems, and water. Government and private sector cooperation on risk protection has gained momentum since the tragedy of September 11, 2001 (9/11).[5]

---

[5]US Department of Homeland Security (DHS), *2009 National Infrastructure Protection Plan.*

We see governments and nongovernmental organizations lumbering to an "all-hazard" risk mitigation model following the missteps of the US Department of Homeland Security before, during, and after Hurricane Katrina. Other international failures to adequately mitigate crises are numerous. Bruce Blythe, chief executive officer of Crisis Management International and author of *Blindsided: A Manager's Guide to Catastrophic Incidents in the Workplace*, anticipated that international standards were underway for improving private sector business continuity and emergency preparedness.[6]

Our opportunity is not merely a matter of satisfying existing or evolving compliance requirements. Indeed, new and emerging risk is seldom covered due to the lagging nature of compliance. Informed choices will be required to improve our holistic chances for resilient self-sufficiency. Those will be qualified by our awareness and readiness to shelter-in-place, evacuate, render first aid, perform search and rescue, and engage our dependents to play their parts. Our ability to mitigate injury and loss and respond nimbly with emergency services, key supply chain recovery, utilities, housing, and jobs requires preparedness. The journey begins with care for people, assets, and critical processes.

My intention with this book is not to write a history of the technical calculation of risk. If that is what you're looking for, I refer you to *Against the Gods* by Peter Bernstein. Bernstein capably chronicles the concept from ancient times through the development of probability and modern insurance concepts.[7]

Nor is it my intention to catalogue the failings of imperiled societies. Neither our hazards nor our solutions are new. I highly recommend Pulitzer Prize winning author Jared Diamond's *Collapse,* which explores "how societies choose to fail or succeed" from the Anasazi to the Vikings. Happily, Diamond's lessons provide more insight for success than doom.[8]

Moisés Naím's *Illicit* will bring the reader up to date with the unintended consequences of globalization and discusses how smugglers,

---

[6]Bruce Blythe of Crisis Management International accurately predicted that NFPA 1600, ASIS All Hazards, and BS 25999-2 for Business Continuity Management would influence preparedness expectations if not certifications. ISO 22399 is also a good reference for preparedness.
[7]Bernstein, *Against the Gods.*
[8]Diamond, *Collapse.*

traffickers, and copycats are hijacking the global economy.[9] Naím, a senior associate in the International Economics Program at the Carnegie Endowment for International Peace, former editor of *Foreign Policy,* executive director at The World Bank, and Venezuelan minister of industry and trade, paints the comprehensive landscape of organized crime's illegal trade for arms, drugs, human beings, information, and money that is undermining legitimate economies and governments by trillions of dollars with our arguable complicity.

In *The Edge of Disaster,*[10] Stephen Flynn comprehensively describes homeland security infrastructure risk for the United States and potentially many other developed countries. His is a persuasive voice for infrastructure overhaul. Flynn's book is a primer for strategic planning and is loaded with the pitfalls of one-time investments, divestitures of maintenance, and critical risk mitigation shortfalls. Flynn, the founding codirector of the George J. Kostas Research Institute for Homeland Security and professor of political science at Northeastern University, examines our current brittle condition and provides insight for its improvement.

I will endeavor to connect the reader to the principal points of risk, mitigation, and return on investment. Security data analysis is more comprehensively illuminated in *Measures and Metrics in Corporate Security: Communicating Business Value* by George Campbell, former chief security officer of Fidelity Investments.[11] Relevant references and additional resources including charts, figures, and maps are intended as visual aids to illustrate concepts. Brief discussion exercises will follow each chapter. All are available for the reader's use within copyright convention at his or her own risk or benefit. Many are scalable for family, small business, community, regional, national, or multinational consideration.

Our collective ability to quantify the benefits of risk mitigation will influence investment in prevention and response preparedness. One institution's success or failure should influence another's. We will learn, hopefully vicariously, from both. Lesson secrecy is a hurdle we must overcome. Hazard recognition and risk mitigation must translate into personal habit, school curricula, and leadership agendas. I trust

[9]Naím *Illicit*
[10]Flynn, *The Edge of Disaster.*
[11]Campbell, *Measures and Metrics in Corporate Security.*

the key points of this book will provoke discussion and continuous risk improvement for all.

Chapter One: The Psychology of Security will enable us to consider our priorities for an effective risk mitigation agenda, beginning with people. We will progress from our own family's protection to larger organizations and communities.

Chapter Two: The Geography of Risk explores our relative capability for applying local risk event mitigation lessons for broader protection of people, assets, and dependent critical process.

Chapter Three: Who's Who in the Zoo? establishes baseline protection prerequisites of identity authentication and access control for both global community commerce and security.

Chapter Four: Prioritizing Risk Mitigation discusses the value of good and best security practices for effective interoperable protection.

Chapter Five: Estimating Return on Security Investment underscores the importance of measuring the total cost risk and benefits in order to meet or exceed stakeholder expectations.

Chapter Six: Leveraging Data to Lead with Good Practices provides context for understanding how we perform in relationship to our peers and against client expectations using benchmarks and surveys.

Chapter Seven: Governance for Sustainability reminds us that our community is the final arbiter of security based on the shared values of the social contract.

Chapter Eight: Resilience revisits the likelihood of critical events and the ability of prepared communities to mitigate or alleviate catastrophic consequences.

Epilogue: How Do We Make Sure This Never Happens Again, Globally? assures us that continuous improvement means the end is only the beginning.

This book is intended to influence a continuing conversation. My apologies are offered in advance to readers who anticipate chronological, linear, or comprehensive recipes for success. Evolving hazards, risk events, and mitigation opportunities occur at many levels and commonly visit from many different directions.

Increasingly resilient communities will require durable vision, mission, and values as compass points to address potential calamity head-on or navigate to avoid or mitigate the collision. They will serve us well each time we are bumped off course and work to recover our heading. Your comments and suggestions supported by relevant data are welcome. They may be sent to contact@securityleader.com.

CHAPTER 1

The Psychology of Security

We set the stage for global risk and community risk mitigation with individuals. Security, like some great coffees, is a blended product of human psychology, critical process, and technology. We begin with the human common denominator. Our awareness and intuition enable constructive mitigations. Abraham Maslow taught us that individuals (and, likely, organizations) are not capable of successful development prior to meeting their primary security needs. Individual human risk must be addressed at home and in the neighborhood in order to focus on larger institutional or community objectives.

Organization and brand reputation rest squarely on both leadership and community's ability to self-protect.

●●●───────────────────────────────────────

Two little girls, 7 and 9, laugh in the bright Carolina sun. They are met by blue sky and a fresh piney woods breeze. The closeness of school and the bus are just behind them. The world is their oyster.

The eggshell blue Pinto appears as a specter in the radiant road heat and exhaust of the departing bus. The driver is intense, like a bad thought on an otherwise promising day. He watches the girls from the crest of the hill. The Pinto tracks their path almost silently on softened warm asphalt. Two adults walk past with dogs in tow.

The Pinto driver pulls within reach, passenger window down, and hesitantly asks the girls for directions. The 9-year-old feels a chill in the air despite the warm afternoon. She instinctively pulls her younger companion close. He gestures that he cannot hear, motioning the girls to come closer.

The 9-year-old thinks: "Why would a man pass two adults to ask directions? Kids don't know directions." She replies aloud: "I don't know, mister . . ." and backs away clutching her smaller friend. The temperature seems to drop precipitously in the Pinto's shadow.

A neighbor drives up to witness this awkward scene. She notes an unheard conversation and the nuance of the girls' retreat. The older girl looks searchingly up the street as if to find an answer. The neighbor senses danger. She intuitively pulls behind the Pinto to record the vehicle's descriptive details.

The Pinto's driver glances furtively in his rearview mirror. He double-checks the witness and slowly drives on, gripping the wheel intently with sweaty palms. He heads northeast to a safe haven 12 miles away, checking his rearview every quarter mile. At his mother's house in Durham, a yellow Pinto is parked next to a brown curtained van with a racked mountain bike. All the vehicles have wired license plates to facilitate quick changes. In the house is a 35 mm camera with a telephoto lens. These are the tools of his trade. He is a hunter of children, thrice convicted.

My wife's frantic telephone call found me at a conference in Annapolis. I could only comprehend fragments in a torrent of words and emotion including "children" and "child molester." The smaller girl was our daughter. I asked in the confusion if the kids were with her. After many agonizing moments she replied, "Yes." I knew we were lucky and said so in an unlikely but hopeful attempt to console her. The irony that I was at a conference attempting to influence the safety of others while my family was in jeopardy did not escape me. My family had intuitively supported my commitment to commuting 180 miles per day in order to reside in a "low crime" community noted for its education resources.

We will be eternally grateful to that older girl and the neighbor who protected our daughter. The event corroborated what crime prevention officers have been telling us for generations: that the community can enable our security or endanger it, depending on our relative risk comprehension and engagement. Personal engagement is crucial to our self-defense and for protecting the community at large.

In this instance, no prosecutable offense had taken place according to the authorities. Nevertheless, we circulated flyers that included photographs of the driver and his vehicles. We recognized the unmitigated risk to the children of our community if the event was not communicated. We reinforced a neighborhood practice of a buddy system for the kids. Departures and arrivals were confirmed by telephone with the assistance of responsible adults.

The flyer content was widely recognized by school bus drivers and others who reported observing our villain loitering adjacent to bus stops and schools. He was arrested weeks later for an unrelated child crime and was remanded to a psychiatric facility for observation. A search by authorities of his bedroom yielded dozens of photographs of little girls resembling our daughter.

We re-substantiated that intuition is an indispensable tool. Our story illustrates risk recognition, response, and mitigation in a simple context. It reminds us that hazards are real and will visit us occasionally despite our best-laid plans. Unusual behavior accompanied by palpable anxiety should warn us. Gavin de Becker memorialized this universal instinct in the *Gift of Fear*.[1] To paraphrase his warning: We all get onto an elevator hundreds of times in the company of strangers without incident. When someone gets on the elevator that makes you feel afraid, get off the elevator. Fight or flight response is in our DNA. Many survivors have depended on it.

Thoughtful risk recognition and awareness of exceptional behavior can potentially help us to avoid individual and institutional hazards as we attempt to protect people and assets of larger communities. My colleague, John Smith, former Group Resilience Director of Prudential plc in the United Kingdom, might offer that failure to consider our options before an event may only induce fright—potentially impairing our ability to act sensibly when the stakes are high. Self-sufficient emergency preparedness should be everyone's goal. We cannot rely solely on the presumed authority for our safety.

1.1 BEGIN AT HOME

There is wisdom in the admonition that "the shoemaker's children should not go barefoot." Those of us who wish to inspire greater preparedness for emergencies must first be prepared at home.

We sometimes learn our way in simple progression. For instance, students of geography get their bearings from their front door, to the neighborhood, community, and world at large. So too, students of risk learn to count on fingers or an abacus long before they operate a calculator or attempt to solve for multiple probabilities. Global security may be regarded as a compound complex equation that requires many subset solutions. We will consider the hazards that may or may not get our attention. If we aim to be protection professionals our understanding of client requirements to protect self and family will serve our purposes when bridging the needs of the community.

---

[1] de Becker, *The Gift of Fear*.

My web search for local public safety information for Seattle, Washington, yielded substantial resources including a community hazards mitigation directory offered by the King County Office of Emergency Management, Washington. See Figure 1.1 for the list of community hazards that have been identified.

Each hazard in this list links to historical event descriptions and instructions for preparedness and response. It is incumbent upon the reader to have timely, updated, and relevant risk information at their fingertips. Federal, county, provincial, and organization internet and intranet resources abound. I encourage researching proven practice resources and communications, including smartphone apps, to meet your needs. Occasionally printing critical information and contact information for inclusion in your emergency preparedness supplies will preclude vital information loss in the event of network failure.

Our ability to communicate risk awareness and mitigation measures that are locally relevant will serve us well when we are tested by a high-risk event. Self and family preparedness are prerequisite building blocks for resilient communities. Risk prevention, suppression, evacuation planning, and insurance coverage are essentials that translate to larger organizations.

Professional first responders, including police, fire, and emergency medical personnel, are trained to prioritize their own safety. Their preparedness also requires confidence that their families are safe or at least conversant and prepared to deal with emergencies. This enables properly trained personnel to report for duty and remain focused on the job without the distraction of unattended risk at home. Public and private sector risk preparedness and mitigation information may be repurposed to diverse audiences. The corporate security team at Cox Enterprises offers intuitive iconographic navigation for its multinational stakeholder group. The *Cox Alert* crisis management site (coxalert.com) serves up preparedness resources for manmade and natural disasters from the Centers for Disease Control and Prevention (CDC), Federal Emergency Management Agency (FEMA), and American Red Cross. It reminds stakeholders that personal security is a shared responsibility that requires preparation. It also links customized crisis communication and resources for need to know managers in a password protected format.

Hazards in King County

- **Avalanches**: An avalanche is a mass of loosened snow or ice that suddenly and swiftly slides down a mountain, often growing as it descends and collects additional material such as mud, rocks, trees, and debris.
- **Dam failures**: There are 87 dams in King County that can impact flood-prone and other areas if they should fail.
- **Droughts**: Drought is a condition of climatic dryness which is severe enough to reduce soil moisture and water below the minimum necessary for sustaining plant, animal, and human life systems.
- **Earthquakes**: An earthquake is a naturally induced shaking of the ground. Earthquakes are caused by the fracture and sliding of rock within the Earth's crust.
- **Fire**: King County experiences three types of fire threats: structure fires, forest fires, and wildland/urban interface fires.
- **Flooding**: A flood is the inundation of normally dry land resulting from the rising and overflowing of a body of water.
- **Hazardous materials releases:** Hazardous materials spills might cause the short- or long-term evacuation of an area.
- **Landslides**: The term landslide refers to the down-slope movement of masses of rock and soil.
- **Pandemic Flu**: A world-wide epidemic involving the spread of a flu virus which human beings have not been exposed to previously.
- **Radiation hazards**: There are a number of potential causes of radiation hazards, such as an accident at a nuclear facility, nuclear detonation, or accident at a research or medical facility utilizing radiological materials.
- **Severe storms**: King County is subject to various local storms that affect the Pacific Northwest throughout the year, such as wind, snow, ice, and hail.
- **Terrorism**: Terrorism has been defined by the FBI as "the unlawful use of force or violence against persons or property to intimidate or coerce a government; the civilian population; or any segment of it, in furtherance of political or social objectives."
- **Transportation accidents**: Transportation available in King County includes air, rail, water, and road. All of these systems provide services on a national, regional, and local basis. A major accident is possible on any of these modes of transportation.
- **Tsunamis/seiches**: Recent studies regarding the potential for a great Cascadia Subduction zone earthquake off the Washington, Oregon, and Northern California coastlines indicate that local tsunami waves may reach nearby coastal communities within minutes of the earthquake.
- **Power and utility outages and energy shortages**: King County's electricity infrastructure includes six hydroelectric plants, four coal-fired plants, and six oil- and natural gas-fired plants.
- **Volcanoes/volcanic eruptions**: Both Mount Rainier and Mount St. Helens are active volcanoes, whose potential eruption could be destructive to our residents, businesses, and infrastructure.

Other natural hazards

- **Extreme heat**
- **Hurricanes**
- **Tornadoes**
- **West Nile Virus**

Figure 1.1 Community Hazards, King County. © 2013 King County. All rights reserved. Used with permission.

1.2 PEOPLE ARE THE TIPPING POINT

Malcolm Gladwell expands our understanding of tipping points where the "momentum for change becomes unstoppable."[2] If indeed sustainable prosperity or even survival depends on unity of purpose, where do we begin? Gladwell's connectors who link us to the world, information specialists who instruct us, and persuaders all influence others. Communities are more likely to move with the momentum of influential individuals who surmise the benefit of their participation. Abraham Maslow said that individuals are capable of developing to their "self actualized" state only after basic physiological, safety, and security requirements are met.[3] See Figure 1.2 for Maslow's hierarchy of needs.

Maslow's hierarchy of needs informs organizational behavior. Alan Chapman, of Businessballs.com (an ethical learning and development resource for people and organizations), depicts Maslow's baseline biological and physiological needs to include air, food, drink, shelter, warmth, sex, and sleep. Safety needs depend on a sense of protection, security, order, law, limits, and stability. Belongingness and love evolve with family, affection, relationships, and work groups. Esteem comes with achievement, status, responsibility, and reputation. When all these needs are met then self-actualization is possible for personal growth

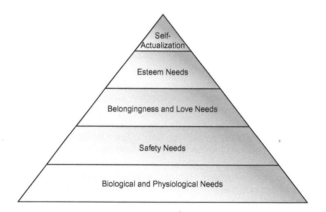

Figure 1.2 Maslow's Hierarchy of Needs.

---

[2]Gladwell, *The Tipping Point.*
[3]Maslow, *Motivation and Personality.*

and fulfillment.[4] When unmet, every member may be required to fend for themselves at the expense of the community. Individuals will be less likely to help others while attending to their own basic needs for survival.

When individual security is assured by a community, the feelings of safety and "belonging" may influence selfless loyalty and the confidence to share resources to overcome community hazards. Attracting, developing, and retaining self-actualized individuals who possess a moral compass and an appreciation for achievement are basic to the interests of self-actualized organizations. This notion is supported by data. Gallup research on engagement suggests that voluntary turnover is affected by an individual's perception of leadership, mission, and sense of caring:

According to Gallup's research, 9 of the 12 workplace elements consistently predict turnover across business units, regardless of an organization's size. These elements are: having clear expectations, having the materials and equipment to do the job right, having the opportunity to do what you do best every day, the belief that someone at work cares, the belief that someone encourages your development, a sense that your opinions count, the mission or purpose of the company making you feel that your job is important, a belief that your coworkers are committed to quality, and having opportunities to learn and grow at work.[5]

In a sense, our loyalty to the institution depends on its loyalty to us. It is conditional.

1.3 BRAND REPUTATION

Successful institutions that have survived multiple generations and proved their resilience despite a myriad of hazards may guide us. James Collins and Jerry Porras write that "built to last" companies are brands guided by their values.[6] Acquisitions and divestitures have muddied corporate identities sufficiently to wobble some data. Are corporate entities even capable of maintaining their identity through cycles of growth and resizing?

---

[4]Chapman, "Abraham Maslow's Hierarchy of Needs Motivational Model."
[5]Robison, "Turning Around Employee Turnover," *Gallup Business Journal*.
[6]Collins and Porras, *Built to Last*.

Sustainable communities and institutions rely on governance under-pinned by shared values and objective principles. Business ventures and not-for-profit organizations are rooted in the value of their product offering. Brand reputation, product perception, and quality assurance are all inexorably linked to care for people who are the stakeholders. See Figure 1.3 for a diagram of brand safety and security risks.

Stakeholder interests will vary from the board of directors to clients and customers. If workers are distracted by their own risks, they may not be focused on the needs of their employers. If consumers cannot confidently and safely obtain a product or service offering, they may not elect to purchase or subscribe. If families and organizations are not aware of risk and response expectations in a disaster, they may seri-ously hamper mitigation efforts and recovery. These are the very real safety and security risks to brand as illustrated in Figure 1.3.

Large organizations sometimes fret about the risks to brand reputa-tion or product quality well before mentioning (almost as an after-thought) that people are their most important asset. My linguistic content teacher Avinoam Sapir would call this an improper social introduction.[7] The intention to unconditionally protect people, assets, and critical processes should proceed in an order that complements incremental security improvement. This mantra does not go unre-warded. It begets brand reputation. Isac Tabib, the accomplished

Figure 1.3 Brand Safety and Security Risks. © Crime Prevention Associates. All rights reserved. Used with permission.

[7]Sapir, "Presenting SCAN—Scientific Content Analysis."

enterprise security systems integrator and innovator, reminded me that the Jews have a prayer that may be repeated three times a day: *A good name is better than good oil.*[8]

Unmitigated risks ultimately affect assets, critical dependent processes, products, services, and brand reputation. Enduring communities including global corporations ought to recognize that people are the tipping point of their everyday existence. Reasonable mitigations of known risks are critical to brand reputation.

Less successful institutions cause anxiety for stakeholders. Maslow's physical and psychological security requirements may segue proportionately to fiscal confidence in today's world of commerce. Interdependent institutions can succeed or fail depending on their risk recognition and response. Integrity cannot be underestimated. One of the more infamous stories of a lack of corporate integrity is the Enron and Arthur Andersen scandal. They were not the only culprits. For many more examples, the U.S. Federal Bureau of Investigation (FBI) keeps a long list of white-collar crime stories on its website: http://www.fbi.gov/news/stories/story-index/white-collar-crime.

Communicating risk with mitigation opportunity is important. Can the sober disclosure of a threat move all to safety in a timely manner? A specific risk like fire may be detected and communicated with warning devices. One hundred percent evacuation of a building will only be likely if the technology is relatively dependable and not prone to false alarm, evacuation drills have been practiced, and self-actualized first responders properly engage to ensure results and compliance. Failure to communicate a precise threat in time or coordinate people, process, and technology with multiple messaging invites haphazard mitigation performance. Hazard recognition and communication is essential to influence effective mitigation.

For example, in 2010 the European Food Safety Authority (EFSA) commissioned a survey of 26,691 individuals from 27 European Union member states to evaluate consumer concern with food safety.[9] Only

---

[8]This phrase refers to a reference in the book of Koheles (Ecclesiastes), which says that "the scent of good oil may precede the oil by a mile or two at most ..." but that "... a good name can precede a person even across continents. (Explanation of the passage comes from "A Good Name Is Better than Good Oil," by Rabbi Yissocher Frand.)
[9]TNS Opinion & Social, "Special Eurobarometer 354."

11 percent of respondents reported permanently changing their eating habits in reaction to a type of food being reported unsafe. Thirty-five percent avoided the food mentioned for a while. Twenty-six percent worried but did nothing. Twenty-four percent ignored the story altogether. This research suggests that the risks to the general population were not effectively recognized, communicated, or mitigated.

Stakeholders, including investors, often expect and require that reasonable care be taken to mitigate risk. Consumer and investor confidence can be rocked or energized by the way a business takes care of its people and dependent communities. Organizational survival requires stakeholder engagement. Investment and divestiture decisions increasingly rely on responsible performance.

1.4 SAFETY AND SECURITY SUSTAINABILITY

Sustainable communities depend on traditions that protect people and assets. Members are held accountable for acts or omissions that are contrary to governing law or policy. Aboriginal Australians may be the only true "built to last" community, having evolved relatively intact for over 40,000 years in a persistently hostile environment.

Tradition requires that Aboriginal grandfathers and grandmothers teach their grandchildren the code for survival including hunting, gathering, cooking, and clothes and tool making. Those who defy the social mores are subject to social sanctions including corporal punishment and ostracism from the community.

Acknowledging families as our root institution and primary social contract is important. Overlapping social and contractual obligations with others will often be superseded by family obligations. Organizational interest in training first responders to assist in emergencies and catastrophic business recovery begins at home with each first responder. If the families are not prepared at home, the likelihood of retaining sufficient numbers of capable volunteers in a regional emergency is low.

Influencing global security is a matter of scale, relying on the self-sufficiency and cooperative assistance of many communities. We must provide ourselves, our families, our governments, and multinational institutions the ability to survive potentially calamitous events. To that end, as students and prospective teachers of risk resilience we will make the case for prevention and mitigation as well as recovery investment. Our experience of catastrophic events will continue. The question before us is: Will we have the where-withal to bounce back? Government and nongovernmental institutions are rising to the challenge with evolving emergency preparedness guidelines.

1.5 WE ARE SURVIVORS

Many of us have survived contagion thanks to inoculation. We have survived other hazards and lived to tell our stories while our equals have suffered graver consequences. I have been shot at, been threatened with a blade, disposed of a letter bomb, and was hit as a pedestrian on a motorway. My family has survived many near misses, too, including the threat of a serial sex offender and an automobile wreck that took us across the path of an oncoming train. We have witnessed hurricanes, tornadoes, and seismic events in close proximity without permanent consequential loss.

Nearly everyone has similar experiences. How do we sustain our outcomes and influence resources for interconnected global communities? How do we enable ourselves and others to prevent or mitigate consequences repeatedly in an affordable, scalable, and sustainable way? Moreover, how do we accomplish these ends efficiently and perhaps just in time in multiple threat scenarios?

William Parrett's lesson of risk avoidance in *The Sentinel CEO* is valuable.[10] He describes how he and others evacuated the World Trade Center during the first terrorist bombing in 1992, never to return again. Parrett and his informed peers influence us to both mind the data and pay attention to our intuition. His team's mindfulness for the value of risk mitigation consequently guided efforts to ensure sustainability at Deloitte Touche Tohmatsu. The tragic impacts of 9/11 were likely similarly mitigated by others who experienced both events. Others were unable to survive despite improved evacuation preparedness and heroism.

Climate change, pandemics, and terrorism periodically get our rapt attention. Paradoxically, many people who worry about these hazards don't have a family emergency plan to cover these and higher probability events such as fire. They also ignore the more frequent risk of

[10]Parrett, *The Sentinel CEO*.

being injured or killed (domestically or overseas) in a transportation accident. Many don't wear seat belts. Results from the Census of Fatal Occupational Injuries (CFOI) program conducted by the US Bureau of Labor Statistics indicated that "transportation accidents accounted for more than two out of every five fatal work injuries in 2011."[11]

Protection professionals are obliged to put the risk data in context for their clients. Successful travel risk mitigation is not solely reliant on seat belt laws and air bags. It is more holistically dependent on the combination of people, process, and technology. Establishing the baseline risk awareness, mitigation capability, and governance within the community is recommended.

Cultures that care empower every member. What is the community duty to protect itself? It's not just the parents' duty to make sure children know the plan and wear seatbelts. Children, friends, neighbors, and professional peers must be expected to remind us when our behavior lapses introduce risk.

Our community communication lines for risk and mitigation must be similarly wide open, two-way, and redundant. Rationalizing a protection program to a family member or a client's understanding of the threat environment is essential. How do we identify extraordinary risk for prioritization? It is essential to ascertain event data and dependent stakeholder opinions. In the 2010 Special Eurobarometer survey concerning food safety (mentioned earlier in this chapter), researchers also asked interviewees about the likelihood of other potential risks happening to them. The percentages of respondents who chose "very likely" or "fairly likely" for the following risks are as follows:

> The economic crisis negatively affecting your life: 66%
> Environmental pollution damaging your health: 61%
> Getting a serious illness: 50%
> The food you eat damaging your health: 48%
> Being injured in a car accident: 44%
> Being a victim of a crime: 33%

The survey respondents potentially overestimate or underestimate the risks depending on survey timing and current awareness or worldview.

[11]Bureau of Labor Statistics, "National Census of Fatal Occupational Injuries."

Clearly we have seen that repetitious reporting of risk phenomena erodes confidence. Most importantly, data is time sensitive. An extended recession with 10 percent incremental dislocation of employment will change both risk perception and reality. We must listen and research. Further education and training may be required to correct misconceptions prior to agreement on a plan. Well-cast surveys may inform security confidence before and after programming. Gaps can be addressed with a re-prioritized understanding of risk to build support for the mitigation agenda. Individual and family emergency plans can be leveraged to cover the basics.

When is an evolving hazard serious enough to warrant our own community action or compel us to warn others? The case for cultural imperatives and our implied duty extends to other security requirements including community access control and critical exception reporting for crime, fire, accidents, or other conditions that threaten people, assets, or process integrity.

We encounter these opportunities to prioritize risk mitigation as we step out the door to our neighborhood and beyond, beginning to understand that other families, communities, and institutions around the world have similar aspirations for safety, security, and prosperity. Our risk mitigation capability will improve incrementally our chances and those of our interconnected neighbors near and far.

Discussion Exercises

1. People are the tipping point. If people are afraid to go to work or school, navigate their neighborhood, or buy products and services, what are the consequences to you and your community?
2. Protect your clients like family and your family like clients. Discuss this proposition and support your view with data.

Additional Information and Resources

1. Child Abduction Resource Center: www.globalmissing.com
2. International Centre for the Prevention of Crime: www.crime-prevention-intl.org
3. National Center for Missing and Exploited Children: www.missingkids.com
4. National Crime Prevention Council: www.ncpc.org
5. NationMaster.com crime statistics: www.nationmaster.com/index.php
6. European Food Safety Authority: www.efsa.europa.eu

●●●───

... The older girl is in medical school. The younger is an honors history major in her junior year at university. The child molester was apprehended and returned to confined psychiatric observation following a brief escape from custody. The numbers of missing and abducted children continue to stagger communities worldwide. According to the United Nations Entity for Gender Equality and the Empowerment of Women, "between 15 and 76 percent of women are targeted for physical and/or sexual violence in their lifetime."[12] Company and institutional risk awareness information ought to be taken home to mitigate shared risks and concerns of all stakeholders and potentially their dependents. All channel hazard reporting should be encouraged inside and outside the organization. Rewards and incentives for information that mitigates risk or establishes accountability for those who harm people enables community protection.

[12]United Nations Entity for Gender Equality and the Empowerment of Women, "Fast Facts."

CHAPTER 2

The Geography of Risk

The relevance of local risk events and lessons learned ought to influence our scalable global protection. The Nisqually earthquake evacuated Starbucks world headquarters for weeks in February 2001. Other lessons came in September and October of that year. The experiences were instructive for the evolution of broader emergency preparedness and business continuity that enabled growth.

Local recognition and understanding of individual security requirements can inform prioritization of regional and global risk mitigation. Individual considerations and community needs may be addressed in the context of just-in-time preparedness. Mapping strategy to stakeholder needs stabilizes organizations and communities. Board level risk can thus be attended as key individuals and constituencies understand their roles.

●●●————————————————————————————

To the casual observer, February 28, 2001 was an exceptionally promising Seattle winter day. Meteorologists were baffled: not a rain cloud was on the horizon and unseasonably mild temperatures were forecast. No specific security risks were on the radar that morning. The Starbucks Support Center tackled the normal protection requirements of a high-growth global coffee company.

Certain geologic forces were about to adjust the outlook. In a place called Nisqually, 57.5 kilometers SSW of Seattle, a 6.8 moment magnitude earthquake sprang from the depths, 52.4 kilometers below the docile surface. It shifted the seismic risk paradigm from a relatively remote regional occurrence in near geologic time to here and now in shockwave speed.

I was on the phone with Pete Rampp seeking assurance for the security equipment supply chain. My priorities changed mid-sentence as I was spun from my seat. The first force wave hit the nine-story square city block headquarters like a fully loaded freight train. I glanced at my clock as it swung on the wall. It was 10:55 a.m. Pacific Standard Time. Pete only heard my uncharacteristically abrupt, "I've got to go," and the tone of the dead connection.

The first concussion seemed to hit from the west as I sought safety in the crumbling office doorway. The hallway wall split and light fixtures blinked and crashed in the swell and roll. I found myself counting aloud

"31 one thousand, 32 one thousand" when a second force seemed to hit from the south. The north wall of the conference room disintegrated in a plaster dust cloud as the building banged against the adjacent parking structure.

That did it for me. At just under a minute with the building still convulsing I navigated the lurching fire escape stairwell three steps at a time for six floors. Inexperienced and untrained for seismic events, including "duck and cover," I relied on the fire evacuation orientation and exited at the front parking lot to witness the general evacuation; narrowly missing the brick and mortar that cascaded from above.

Within 30 minutes, more than 2,000 employees, service personnel, and visitors nervously awaited instructions in the parking lot. Cell phone service disappeared, sparking rumors of a regional disaster. Structural stability confirmation for bridges and buildings takes time to assess. I advised Rick Arthur, my boss, and Orin Smith, the CEO, that no serious physical injuries were yet reported.

Facilities immediately undertook the structural assessment of the building with the landlord and the city. Protection personnel surveyed the windows from all sides with binoculars, looking for people who may have had their escape obstructed as first responders were arriving. Information Technology brought up their plan for an orderly shutdown of the network. General re-entry was out of the question pending damage reports. The Partner and Asset Protection (P&AP) team made provisions for additional 24/7 security personnel to cover access control issues.

2.1 ASSESSING PRIORITIES AND THE STRATEGIC GAME PLAN

The building performed admirably during one of the state of Washington's largest seismic events. Foundational shock absorbers helped protect against serious structural damage. Swinging lights had severed fire suppression sprinkler heads, dousing the building in hundreds of tons of water. Within hours, senior leadership and designated critical personnel began mapping a building recovery process that would take months to clear water damage, replace fixtures, and advance the building to higher seismic standards.

Workarounds were required for networked critical processes including payroll, accounts payable, and automated retail ordering for stores. Supplemental processes were prioritized or innovated for recovery where existing plans fell short. The Starbucks Support Center suffered a great amount of non structural damage that could not be repaired for total re-occupancy until September.

Risk appreciation is a sobering phenomenon. The Nisqually earthquake was a relevant "near miss" event for Seattle. It allowed calculated appreciation for the mitigation previously accomplished and nimble management of support groups that could rise to the occasion when needed to deliver the promises of mission and values. It also fueled an expanded understanding that potential single points of failure could threaten the ability to recover. Nisqually also expedited larger considerations for comprehensive prevention, emergency preparedness, emergency management, and business continuity strategies. Risk reassessment and mitigation investment reprioritization are always required for continuous improvement.

Earthquakes are relatively predictable phenomena around the world within near geologic time. Seismologists and at least one computer model agree that a similar shift a bit closer to the city center could wreak considerably more devastation. A potential future Seattle fault line shift at a conservative force of 6.7 would likely kill 1,600 persons, injure 24,000, and displace 45,000 families. The epicenter of destruction would be uncomfortably close—damaging 10,000 commercial buildings and houses.[1] These implications drove business continuity and other risk mitigation investments for facilities, networks, and, most importantly, people, safety, and security.

The results of a more recent Society for Human Resource Management survey confirm that security and safety in the workplace are considered "important" or "very important" to their job satisfaction by nearly all workers (90%).[2] Similarly, Gallup research has shown that if there is a perception that leadership allows hazards to go unattended, employees will leave.[3] People who are afraid to be at work tend to feel underappreciated, uncared for, and underpaid. The combination of physical and economic safety concerns can impact loyalty, honesty, and the engagement required for customer service and product quality.

Following the earthquake evacuation, cross-functional recovery managers determined other dependencies in rapid order. Many left their purses, wallets, credit cards, checkbooks, personal identification, keys, and laptops in a building that was for all intents and purposes inaccessible. The stories of inconvenience and anguish ranged from an

[1]Daughton, "Pinpointing Devastation."
[2]Society for Human Resource Management (SHRM). "2012 Employee Job Satisfaction."
[3]Harter, Schmidt, and Keyes, "Well-Being in the Workplace."

inability to get home to impairments for banking, bill paying, and even grocery purchases. International travelers including consultants and visitors left behind tickets, itineraries, and passports. One unfortunate woman had abandoned her bridal gown.

Pressing asset transfers, contracts, research, lease agreements, and projects in progress were potentially at risk without a stout recovery effort. Retrieval of critical business items including passwords and personal belongings were prioritized. Requests for recovery were triaged by P&AP and expedited over weeks when access was limited to hard hat-equipped P&AP and facilities personnel.

It was later learned that during the quake a maintenance engineer had been changing bulbs for the Starbucks Siren icon. The Siren sits dramatically above First Avenue South, 12 stories above Starbucks Center, a crowned goddess enchanting every visitor and passerby with the alchemy of coffee. One can only imagine the poor fellow's ride atop that ladder. Her twisted steel frame evidenced the force that was conducted throughout the building.

Nearly all appreciated their luck. There were no critical injuries. On any other winter day an evacuation into a freezing rain could have suffered the consequences of exposure and hypothermia. Fortune also provided the recently vacated 25,000 square foot roasting plant five blocks away. It was still robustly connected to the existing network. An unsecured primary server tipped over by the rocking was set upright, rebooted, and operated as if nothing happened. Critical recovery operations were relatively unhindered by space or technology constraints.

The trauma of the event revisited some as traumatic events often do. More near misses could have had serious consequences. Many sensed the anxiety of re occurrence. More than a few expressed doubts about returning to the building. Counseling, open forums, and building tours addressed many fears. The company demonstrated that it cared. Continuous messaging and workarounds ensured uninterrupted payroll, store inventory distribution, and a prioritized recovery of the building. Communications kept affected personnel informed on a range of issues from personal property recovery requests to ongoing seismic risk. Counselors were brought in to advise and assist the traumatized.

Existing severe weather communication lines along with web sites, voice mail, and e-mail options were leveraged for relevant situation updates along with local market television messaging. A "tell, show, do" approach let the community know that all anxieties would be addressed. Rick Arthur, vice president of administration, and Orin Smith, the CEO, detailed building safety and refurbishing at open forums. Cross-functional teams stabilized the people tipping point through mitigation (see Figure 2.1).

Left to their own purposes people will take care of themselves and family first. Unengaged individuals may misinterpret that the organization is moving on without them if they don't know the plan. "Non critical" personnel may move on without informative communications, causing a talent loss that impairs long-term recovery, particularly if risk perception is unimproved. Leadership that anticipates and mitigates anxiety with thoughtful incremental messaging engages productive behavior by clarifying communication channels and reconnects separated individuals back to the community recovery plan.

Connecting the details of event mitigation back to the cultural priorities of people care, asset protection, and critical process recovery serves as a shock absorber to allow individuals to process their value to the community.

The dependencies on people for critical processes, from banking transactions to inventory management and payroll, were newly appreciated.

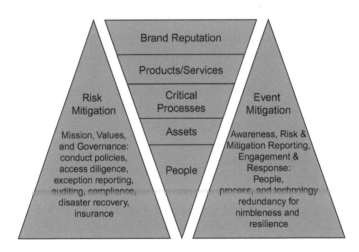

Figure 2.1 Stabilizing the Tipping Point. © Crime Prevention Associates. All rights reserved. Used with permission.

Near single points of failure were added to the mitigation list for improvements. Key personnel were fatigued 72 hours after the quake. Service provider assistance mitigated potential burnout. Access control and premises security were passed to trusted service providers as building recovery operations were prioritized. Pre-positioning redundancy and services is a key consideration for business recovery and continuity of operations.

The Nisqually earthquake was a defining moment for many. Community morale and reputation were enhanced with every effort to care for people and make them feel safe again. Starbucks relied on its primary principle to provide a great work environment with respect and dignity. As with the triple murder in Washington, D.C., in 1997, honest conversations took place regarding ongoing risk and mitigation.

2.2 ALL-HAZARDS MITIGATION

Meeting and exceeding expectations for security and safety concerns can galvanize the community for greater investments. Starbucks was not content to merely reoccupy the building and restore processes to pre-event conditions. Leadership was determined to substantially improve both the facilities and risk mitigation capabilities. Emergency Response was evolving to Business Continuity as the result of cross-functional research and engagement.

Starbucks Center personnel and contractors welcomed the improvements that reaffirmed their choice of employment or assignment. Visitors seemed to appreciate a building orientation with emergency exit and seismic information that introduced many meetings along with a coffee tasting. Without mitigation, risk can wobble the foundation of the community, affecting people's confidence and ability to perform critical processes, produce quality product, deliver services, and maintain stakeholder confidence. Care, on the other hand, expresses values including commitment.

Innovation and teamwork accomplished process workarounds that guaranteed product to the stores. To the outside world, the effect of the Nisqually earthquake on Starbucks was a nonevent. Brand reputation survived intact because of good fortune and commitment to people. Inside Starbucks, the Nisqually quake shook additional realities into emergency preparedness. For instance, if the Seattle Fault line shifted with equal force, the needs would reach well beyond what the local public emergency first responders could provide. The 2,500 people in the headquarters parking lot could not be bystanders.

True emergency response and business recovery required a comprehensive plan and a cadre of self-actualized responders. Ideally, Community Emergency Response Team (CERT) trained and equipped personnel could provide for building evacuation, structural assessment, first aid, and search and rescue.[4] Scalable sustainability had to be developed with local capability worldwide. An expanding footprint promised more hazards. Although many had not yet imagined the likelihood of pervasive terrorism or pandemic prior to the 9/11 and "Amerithrax" attacks, the need to deal globally with both natural and manmade catastrophic events had become clear.[5]

Extended markets, supply chains, and networks require protection. Understanding global risk and mitigating it in a locally relevant fashion presumed a broader effort. Security and political risks are routinely forecasted by governments and private sector enterprises to inform constituencies from citizens to client organizations on the relative hazards of travel, business continuity, or expansion. Figure 2.2 is an example of a global security and political risks map developed by Control Risks, an independent global risks consultancy. It depicts hazards in color from insignificant (white) to low (pale green), medium (orange), high (red), and extreme (crimson).

Control Risks' ratings assess the likelihood of risk by calculating the impact of a wide range of factors including theft, injury to employees, kidnapping, damage to installations, information theft, fraud, extortion, expropriation of assets, and loss of control to an organization's assets in a particular country. Conditions may vary greatly between cities or provinces within the same region depending on local

---

[4]The Community Emergency Response Team (CERT) program is made available through FEMA (http://www.fema.gov/community-emergency-response-teams). Citizen Corps educates people about disaster preparedness and provides training for skills such as fire safety, light search and rescue, team organization, and disaster medical operations (http://www.ready.gov/citizen-corps). The *Are You Ready?* guide provides a step-by-step approach to disaster preparedness by informing readers about local emergency plans, how to identify hazards that affect their local area, and how to develop and maintain an emergency communications plan and disaster supplies kit (http://www.ready.gov/are-you-ready-guide).

[5]The FBI provides a detailed history of the anthrax attacks that began in the United States immediately following the 9/11 terrorist attacks: http://www.fbi.gov/about-us/history/famous-cases/anthrax-amerithrax. Five people were killed and 17 became sick when they opened pieces of mail that contained the deadly anthrax spores.

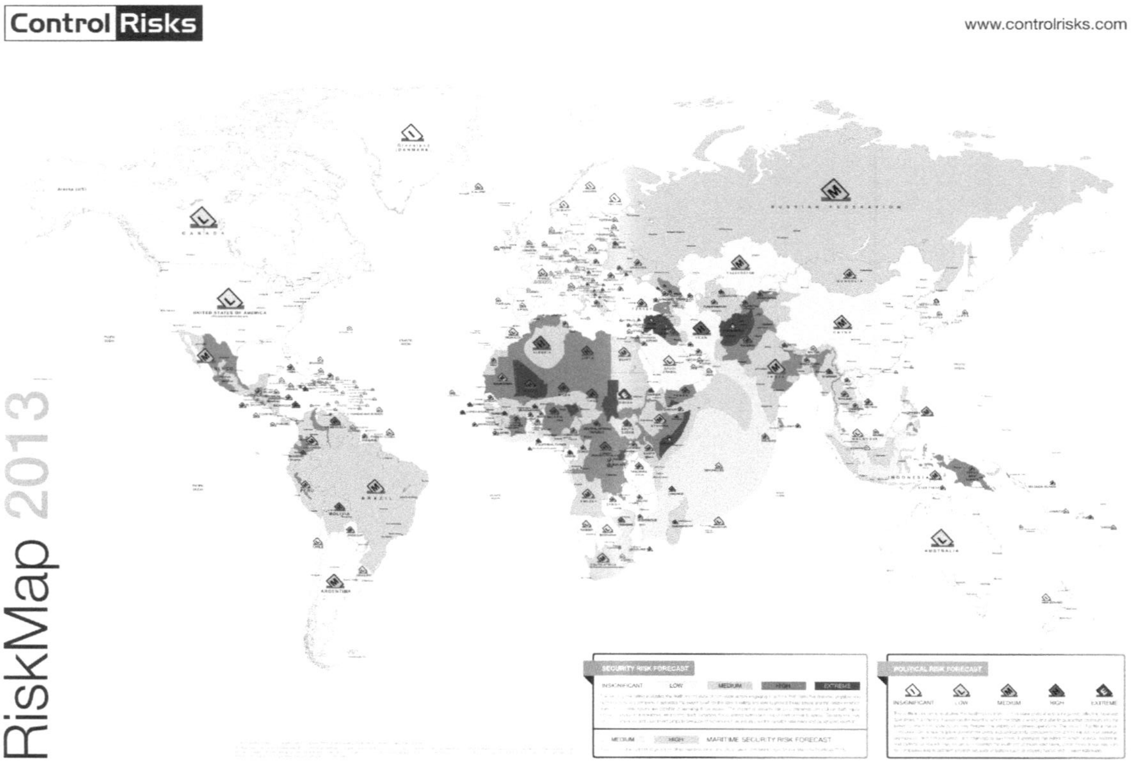

Figure 2.2 Risk Map. © Control Risks Group Limited. All rights reserved. Used with permission.

situations. Organizations or institutions with global dependencies may require virtual risk information, including climate conditions if they are dependent on products from a certain region. Other risk probabilities for maritime security, such as piracy (shaded gray in Figure 2.2), must also be considered to design all-hazard risk mitigation.

Known terrorist operations shape the risk landscape and shade the mapping. Multinational terrorist operations continue to garner attention post 9/11. Coalition allies, including businesses and private citizens, remain targets for violence. Figure 2.3 is an illustration of known security threats patterns by country. Multinational terrorist operations continue to garner attention post-9/11. Coalition allies, including businesses and private citizens, remain targets for violence.

Orientation by maps and relevant data enables the student of global risk to understand the multidimensional nature of risk including the

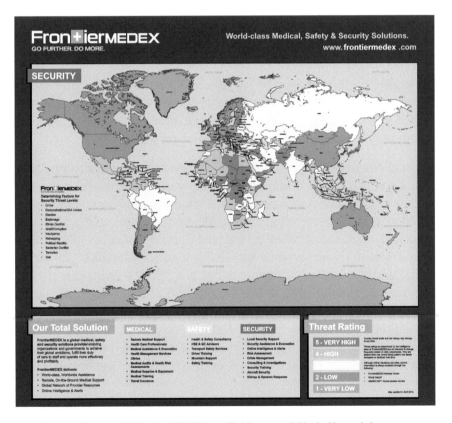

Figure 2.3 Threat Map. © 2013 FrontierMEDEX Inc. All rights reserved. Used with permission.

Figure 2.4 Washington DC and London Crime. © 2008 CAP Index. All rights reserved. Used with permission.

propensity for some hazards to traverse nominal political borders. Discrete information, including breaking news, can be detailed and imaged for catastrophic events, evolving threats, and environmental conditions to enable nimble preparation or response.

Local risk specificity is also easily depicted to highlight comparative data. Crime incidence is mapped in many parts of the world by responsible law enforcement organizations. Crime information, including sex offender data, is increasingly available to the public. In addition to municipal criminal incidence, indexed data is also available from private sector resources such as CAP Index for Canada, the United States, and the United Kingdom.[6] The CAP Index represents the risk of crime on a scale of 0 to 2,000 with 100 representing the average incidence for United States census track or United Kingdom ward population data (see Figure 2.4). Relative risk warrants a deeper dive for conditions and mitigation requirements when relevant hazards threaten community activity. Proprietary crime reporting offers

---

[6]Visit the CAP Index website to create customized crime reports of any address, neighborhood, or area in the United States, Canada, or United Kingdom: http://www.capindex.com/.

additional trend information that indicates actual crime experience. Broad implementation of robust security mitigation measures may guard against hazard conditions that change or travel from adjacent boundaries. Crime data instructs risk for local market hazards.

2.3 JUST-IN-TIME PREPAREDNESS

Post-9/11 and prior to the D.C. sniper and Tube bombing events that occurred in 2002 and 2005, respectively, Starbucks P&AP mapped "tier one" homeland security (high risk) cities, including Washington, D.C., and London, replete with coffee store locations, offices, and distribution points. This allowed calculation of risk adjacencies and business continuity contingencies for both events. Brand ubiquity requires nimble adaptation for global risk. Government and private sector intelligence can mitigate the same threats.

Unplanned events will also occur. Specific and incidental risk will vary. On September 11, 2001, many global and local organizations operated in the shadow of the World Trade Center or near the Pentagon. Adjacency to both Wall Street and the military, the professed specific targets of Al-Qaeda, put all in harm's way.

Specific threats, adjacencies, and incidental risk may be anticipated. Knowing your neighbor's risk and emergency plan may be beneficial, particularly when accidents or acts of sabotage have potentially devastating collateral effects. Adjacencies to atomic facilities or petrochemical processors may inform risk and mitigation planning differently than those for icons, mass transit hubs, or other infrastructure targets. Knowing risk mitigation particulars and incorporating them into your plan will potentially inform evacuation or shelter-in-place options.

Communities that care share risk information to enable their constituents. Those in need can sometimes galvanize news agencies, police, politicians, and local citizens groups to action. The birth of the World Wide Web and the resulting speed of communication aids preparedness and response. The web, along with other broadcast media including radio and television, may be leveraged for just-in-time awareness and mitigation. As an additional risk calculation, the web has also played a role in terror orchestration, as have other telecommunications networks. It may serve to bear in mind that all infrastructure

Figure 2.5 Security Operations Center. © Diebold, Inc. All rights reserved. Used with permission.

networks are subject to attack, compromise, or overload. Communications redundancy is recommended.

Ideally, mitigation information for known hazards should be shared prior to predictable emergencies. CERT training is one example. The concept of "Three days three ways" enables personnel and their families to anticipate the need for 72 hours worth of food, water, and emergency needs for home, work, and evacuation contingencies.[7]

Proliferation of post-incident information should occur on all available channels. It is often impaired by telecommunication network overload. Pre-event information dissemination and redundancies may hedge this shortfall. Security operations centers (SOCs) allow networked, redundant broadcast and Internet-enabled news and intelligence. An artist's rendition appears in Figure 2.5.

[7] "The 3 Days 3 Ways Disaster Preparedness Workbook," developed by the King County Office of Emergency Management and the American Red Cross, projects a very simple message to the residents of King County, Washington: be prepared to survive on your own for a minimum of three days following a disaster. For large disasters, government assistance may not be available for up to seven days. The three ways to become prepared include: making a plan, building a kit, and getting involved (http://www.xmarksthesound.org/pdfs/).

The concept depicted in figure 2.5 is a four-operator console with flat screens and an interactive whiteboard for project development or crisis management. SOCs may simultaneously connect to numerous peripheral platforms to follow evolving risk events, ensure access control, track travelers, and monitor security services. Single platform integration can offer value-added capability including enterprise-wide emergency status communications, alarm monitoring, virtual video surveillance or event corroboration, exception detection, and investigation development. The objective is to ascertain risk conditions for stakeholders, facilities, and their respective communities worldwide while deterring or impacting criminal activity and its related cost.

Subscription mapping software products can illustrate reported events within existing retail market, manufacturing, and supply chain coordinates with travel information. The idea is to globally discern, at a glance, all hazards for business operations, suppliers, networks, and travelers. Nimble risk appreciation allows reaction to prevailing and evolving conditions that affect people, product, and process. Facility access control and interactive security systems can confirm both video and audio emergency event conditions. Operators may ascertain adjacent critical events ranging from reported crimes of violence to ecological accidents or terror strikes in order to determine risk for employee, customer, guest, or other stakeholders.

Risk reporting information may be shared by networked communications, mail, wallet cards, or on pay envelopes that are delivered weekly or biweekly around the globe. Local police, fire, and ambulance notifications will likely supersede other reporting requirements that are imposed by operating policy.

As we will see in Chapter Seven, governance rules may address a "duty to report" injury, damage, theft and/or threats, or conditions that may risk injury, damage, or theft. E-mail, instant messaging, and other interactive reporting methodologies may support the social contracts or policies adopted by the community. Every communicated risk condition requires current reporting contacts and network addresses to leverage data distribution for awareness, response, program reporting metrics, and improvement.

Worst-case scenarios will potentially feature a failing utility grid, precluding recharging peripheral devices. Security methodology must inform the client community of risk and enable condition reporting. Effective protection is layered and integrated for both risk detection and response. Routine processes and communications contacts must be printed in anticipation of grid and digital network failures.

Integration of virtual event notification and communications allows key personnel to be advised globally of evolving risks with hazard-specific mitigation for prevailing weather, health, security, and safety conditions.[8] Integrated capabilities allow condition advisories before, during, and after a trip. Simple mitigations range from trip timing to postponement. Mobile communications allow awareness of spontaneous and evolving hazards. Providers like Dialogic (www.dialogic.com) and Send Word Now (www.sendwordnow) link emergency and non-emergency global communications for their clients. More complex traveler aid may range from safe haven advisories and medical referrals up to country evacuation and repatriation.

2.4 MAPPING STRATEGY TO STAKEHOLDER REQUIREMENTS

At Avon Products, Bob Littlejohn surveyed his leadership for "what kept them awake at night." The list included natural disasters, pandemics, terrorism, product extortion, corruption, workplace violence, information security, and the insider threat. These risks were further developed with supporting intelligence provided by the US State Department's Overseas Advisory Council (OSAC) and others. Organization-specific threat assessment and communication are the logical step after ascertaining the public sector view.

Littlejohn's pragmatic risk approach to the private sector was seasoned by his years in command at the New York City Police Department and the New York City Office of Emergency Management. Willard Rappleye chronicled Littlejohn's achievements as a volunteer leader for the International Security Manager's Association (ISMA) and as vice president for global security for Avon Products.[9] Bob is credited with early efforts to coordinate chief security officer risk communications between government and the private sector post-9/11.

[8] International SOS (www.internationalsos.com/) helps organizations ensure the health and security of their travelers and employees around the world.
[9] Rappleye Jr., "Thrust and Counterthrust."

Management increasingly recognizes the requirement for competent security leadership. William Parrett, CEO of Deloitte Touche Tohmatsu, asserts the value of security leadership: "Central to the creation and sustained development of a culture of risk management is the chief security officer." Parrett makes the case for setting the tone at the top. The community recognizes that leadership cares. Risk awareness and security mitigation are required disciplines for all. A sense of duty and the concept of the community "social contract" are essential.

Parrett's underlying message to CEOs is that management, including boards of directors, cannot have a laissez faire attitude toward risk. The hazard landscape is too harrowing. The compliance environment after Enron and Sarbanes-Oxley requires more accountability. After the economic meltdown of 2008 and 2009, it will be more robust than ever. Current and evolving government requirements for emergency preparedness and business continuity will likely also hold leadership increasingly responsible for acts and omissions that fail to protect people and assets. To that end, the Security Executive Council, a problem-solving research and services organization, undertook the enumeration of board-level security risks (see Figure 2.6).[10] The hazards and security mitigation opportunities ought to interest stakeholders for any responsible organization.

As you can see in Figure 2.6, potential risks are numerous. Actual and vicarious experience within an industry segment or the public or private sector may inform your mindset. Failure to reasonably anticipate, prevent, or mitigate may introduce sanctions ranging from civil and criminal culpability to loss of insurance due to negligence.

Mapping risk relevant, breakthrough security goals and tactics three to five years out is a beneficial exercise for broadening security risk mitigation and ensuring resilience of new or maturing protection programs.

Our risk mitigation agendas will be longer than our careers. Connecting persuasively to the organization culture, strategy, and principal ambitions of the community is the key to our relevance and sustainability. Authenticating members of the community will likely be a

---

[10]Board-level risk is an industry-neutral research product, representing an amalgamation of diverse risk assessments.

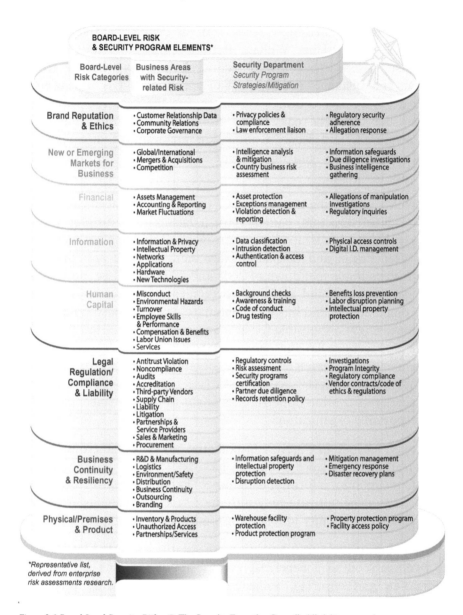

BOARD-LEVEL RISK & SECURITY PROGRAM ELEMENTS*			
Board-Level Risk Categories	Business Areas with Security-related Risk	Security Department *Security Program Strategies/Mitigation*	
Brand Reputation & Ethics	• Customer Relationship Data • Community Relations • Corporate Governance	• Privacy policies & compliance • Law enforcement liaison	• Regulatory security adherence • Allegation response
New or Emerging Markets for Business	• Global/International • Mergers & Acquisitions • Competition	• Intelligence analysis & mitigation • Country business risk assessment	• Information safeguards • Due diligence investigations • Business intelligence gathering
Financial	• Assets Management • Accounting & Reporting • Market Fluctuations	• Asset protection • Exceptions management • Violation detection & reporting	• Allegations of manipulation investigations • Regulatory inquiries
Information	• Information & Privacy • Intellectual Property • Networks • Applications • Hardware • New Technologies	• Data classification • Intrusion detection • Authentication & access control	• Physical access controls • Digital I.D. management
Human Capital	• Misconduct • Environmental Hazards • Turnover • Employee Skills & Performance • Compensation & Benefits • Labor Union Issues • Services	• Background checks • Awareness & training • Code of conduct • Drug testing	• Benefits loss prevention • Labor disruption planning • Intellectual property protection
Legal Regulation/ Compliance & Liability	• Antitrust Violation • Noncompliance • Audits • Accreditation • Third-party Vendors • Supply Chain • Liability • Litigation • Partnerships & Service Providers • Sales & Marketing • Procurement	• Regulatory controls • Risk assessment • Security programs certification • Partner due diligence • Records retention policy	• Investigations • Program Integrity • Regulatory compliance • Vendor contracts/code of ethics & regulations
Business Continuity & Resiliency	• R&D & Manufacturing • Logistics • Environment/Safety • Distribution • Business Continuity • Outsourcing • Branding	• Information safeguards and intellectual property protection • Disruption detection	• Mitigation management • Emergency response • Disaster recovery plans
Physical/Premises & Product	• Inventory & Products • Unauthorized Access • Partnerships/Services	• Warehouse facility protection • Product protection program	• Property protection program • Facility access policy

Representative list, derived from enterprise risk assessments research.

Figure 2.6 Board-Level Security Risks.

primary conditional requirement of the social contract prior to receiving its benefits and protection. The risk of counterfeit credentials and false identities to people, assets, and critical processes are consequential to every agenda.

Discussion Exercise

How do you make your clients aware of risk with relevant mitigation information? Have you developed a community emergency response team? Detail local and regional risks, resources, your plan, and a recommended survival kit for your community.

Additional Information and Resources

1. *Blindsided: A Manager's Guide to Catastrophic Incidents in the Workplace* by Bruce Blythe
2. IS 317: Introduction to Community Emergency Response Teams (CERT), an independent study course offered through FEMA's Emergency Management Institute, for those wanting to complete training or as a refresher for current team members (http://www.fema.gov/community-emergency-response-teams/training-materials).
3. "Preparing for the Unexpected," 5th edition, by the Commonwealth of Australia's Attorney-General's Department: http://www.em.gov.au.
4. Public Safety Canada: http://www.publicsafety.gc.ca/.
5. UK Cabinet Office's Emergency Response and Recovery Guidance: https://www.gov.uk/emergency-response-and-recovery.
6. "Disaster Preparedness for People with Disabilities," by the American Red Cross and FEMA: http://www.redcross.org/prepare/location/home-family/disabilities.
7. "Knowledge Corner: Business Continuity," the Security Executive Council: https://www.securityexecutivecouncil.com/knowledge/index.html?mlc = 603.
8. *Business Continuity Playbook*, edited by Dean Correia: http://store.elsevier.com/product.jsp?isbn = 9780124116481.

... the Nisqually quake experience prompted funding for a formal business continuity resource. It was put into action in 2005 when hundreds of stores and thousands of Starbucks employees were adversely affected before, during, and after Hurricane Katrina, the US Gulf Coast "storm of the century." Each was accounted for despite the complications of regional evacuations. What are known as "CUP" funds at Starbucks were designated for partner catastrophic assistance, and along with Social Responsibility's commitment of millions of dollars, the company enabled personal and regional recovery efforts.

China leadership was similarly guided during Starbucks' response to the catastrophic earthquake of May 2008. Reported deaths exceeded 69,000 with several hundred thousand injuries and millions of homes lost.

Like Katrina, all personnel were accounted for by the local crisis management team. Many suffered loss or injury of family members, homes, and untold emotional distress. In addition to assisting physical and emotional needs, substantial funding seeded contributions targeted for the recovery of schools.

CHAPTER 3

Who's Who in the Zoo?

Integrated identity authentication and access control are fundamental requirements for sustainable risk mitigation. A layered and integrated program can arguably protect people, assets, and critical process to enable global commerce or service delivery with sustainable security. Perimeter access control in physical and networked logical spaces requires identity confirmation and exception reporting. People, data, and goods may either operate within the policy and standards of the community or be blocked pending compliance. Insider and outsider risks are visited along with supply chain and other mitigation opportunities.

●●●————————————————————————————————

R.H. selected "file" then "print" and with two mouse clicks capped the largest project of her career. The invoice purred from her laser jet printer. The service payment of $268,000 marked another milestone for the intrepid applications manager.

She had applied herself diligently if not compulsively to this project, wheeling the halls with a sense of urgency in her red motorized cart. She delivered invoices and check requests by hand. She charmed and wheedled others to advance her cause.

Checks were provided to her personally to meet deadlines and avoid the inconvenience posed by the slow pace of control processes and the US mail. Her consultant appreciated the consideration. So did R.H. They were one and the same.

Her manager arrived at my office on my birthday. Like most late Friday afternoon surprises, the news was not good. He surmised that, "We might have a problem in suspicious expenses." He did not suspect that most of the damage had occurred in capital accounts. Conversion to an Oracle system temporarily delayed reporting activity and neutralized a robust control for fraud protection.

R.H. had happily left the building earlier in the day with another check in hand. She was reportedly on her way to a family vacation in Alaska. Marc Osborn, the compliance manager, confirmed concern of further damage when he reported that $3.7 million had either been issued to or requested for the consultant. Marc's vendor account inquiry documented the processed check requests.

The company stopped payment on the most recent check and blocked R.H.'s access to both the building and the network to mitigate additional loss. Like many defalcations and embezzlements, this one might have been mitigated with earlier detection. It was not the first time she had stung an employer. The screening process would have revealed her misstatements and omissions of employment history if the record had included the prior activity excluded by the court.

Simple check request and payment control violations must be reported. Exception reporting would have revealed that the consultant was both an increasingly high frequency and high dollar invoice payee for multiple reporting periods.

There were also telltale lifestyle indicators unknown to management. According to others, R.H. appeared to be doing very well. Luxury cars, real estate, and other acquisitions gave the appearance that she was being rewarded for uncommon accomplishments. In reality her project performance was lacking, but no single person had sufficient information to connect the dots.

Mitigating actions prevented additional loss and paved the way for asset recovery. The case was simultaneously reported to local and federal law enforcement agencies. Law and Corporate Affairs initiated civil action to seize her assets. Phil Hummel, compliance director, coordinated the eventual auction of homes, boats, and more than 30 vehicles, ranging from vintage Mercedes to "his and her" Harleys....

Access control diligence can ideally be performed on a pre-employment or preassignment basis with identity verification and reputation diligence. The expedited denial of R.H.'s access to the facilities and network was too late to prevent the loss. Blocking her access did mitigate a worse outcome by preserving critical evidence for both the criminal prosecution and restitution. Her voice mail request for an administrative coordinator to delete incriminating files coupled with videotaped attempts to reenter the building and the network demonstrated her intent.

Closer inquiry into R.H's employment history by law enforcement evidenced previously undetectable omissions and falsifications. A previous felony theft had been adjudicated and effectively expunged from the public record, thus confusing any prospective employer's routine background check. A more transparent employment history could have precluded an employment offer. Upon discovering her scheme, compensatory actions allowed recovery of assets just short of the total loss.

Sustainable security begins with access control. Dependable identity authentication and exception reporting capabilities are required to ensure profitability and mission performance. Experience, benchmarked good practices, as well as state, provincial, regional, national, and international compliance conventions guide us. They serve to authenticate trusted agents and transactions in both the physical and cyber environments.

Figure 3.1 depicts identity authentication as a first order of business for access control. Lowest common denominator credentials include government-issued photographic identification. Although currently challenged with counterfeiting and identity fraud, governments are moving to improve credentials. Access permission qualification will ideally occur with a knowledge-based screening, in which the credential applicant must affirmatively identify personal protected data including social security or insurance numbers, previous telephone exchanges, addresses, etc. to authenticate themselves as the true identity owner.

Curriculum vitae (CV) diligence demands corroboration of education and certification credentials along with employment history and other applicant claims. Undetected fabrication of professional experience and capability is as potentially detrimental to an organization's reputation as the losses that may follow. Negligent hiring and retention are not within stakeholder expectations.

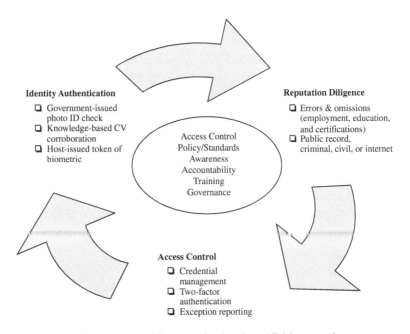

Identity Authentication
- ❑ Government-issued photo ID check
- ❑ Knowledge-based CV corroboration
- ❑ Host-issued token of biometric

Reputation Diligence
- ❑ Errors & omissions (employment, education, and certifications)
- ❑ Public record, criminal, civil, or internet

Access Control Policy/Standards Awareness Accountability Training Governance

Access Control
- ❑ Credential management
- ❑ Two-factor authentication
- ❑ Exception reporting

Figure 3.1 Access Control Continuum. © Crime Prevention Associates. All rights reserved.

A biometric token or access credential for facilities and logical systems should only be assigned after performing reputation diligence. Once access is approved systems should be equipped to report exception activity within the acceptable use standards of the organization. The process ideally will reoccur. Previously approved trusted agents should be recertified on a scheduled basis, promotion, or change in assignment.

Integrated access control with true identity management and exception reporting is perhaps the most effective approach to security that reasonable organizations might endeavor to undertake. Good and best practices for both physical and information security are enumerated in existing and evolving compliance requirements including ISO standards. Organization and brand reputations rest squarely on an entity's ability to protect people, assets, and critical dependent processes. Counterintuitively, many of today's screening and diligence processes may cost more than may be required for actual identity authentication. Importantly, existing practices may merely corroborate false or stolen information.

3.1 INSIDER AND OUTSIDER RISKS

Business partners often pose the greatest risk for security breaches. "Insider risk" mitigation recognizes that enabling untrustworthy agents is hazardous to people and assets. Employees and service providers are routinely given access to people, assets, and information without effective identity authentication and reputation diligence. Failure to demonstrate diligence in hiring and assignment may risk more than injury or asset loss. Additional legal liabilities and compliance shortfalls may occur.

Businesses operating in the United States and globally can be subject to fines and imprisonment such as multiplier penalties under the Federal Sentencing Guidelines or similar international requirements when adequate security controls including awareness, prevention, detection, and reporting systems are not in place to preclude or mitigate crime.[1]

---

[1]United States Sentencing Commission, "Guidelines Manual," 488, According to the manual "Organizations can act only through agents and, under federal criminal law, generally are vicariously liable for offenses committed by their agents. Convicted individual agents of organizations are sentenced in accordance with the guidelines and policy sanctions ... [to] provide just punishment, adequate deterrence, and incentives for organizations to maintain internal mechanisms for preventing, detecting, and reporting criminal conduct."

Most risk vulnerability assessments will reveal that poorly designed access may result in injury to people and diversion, corruption, or damage to assets including information. According to the US Bureau of Labor Statistics, one half of large employers reported a violent assault in 2005. Coworkers accounted for 34 percent of those incidents.[2] Estimated direct fraud costs, to US businesses alone, were reported at $652 billion for 2006.[3] For the global market, the Association of Certified Fraud Examiners (ACFE) found that businesses lose, on average, five percent of their revenues annually. In 2011, that translated to $3.5 trillion lost to fraud worldwide.[4] Large percentages of injury and loss are preventable or mitigatable with diligent screening, risk awareness, access control, exception reporting, and timely response.

The risk of placing a serial sex offender in a school environment is obvious. So too is assigning a practiced fraudster in a bank. The risk may be less obvious when the ineffectively screened person has access to people or assets outside his or her immediate domain. Adjacent targets like a child care center in a remote part of a multiuse building or a human resource data center require protection. Acceptable use standards must allow access only on a need-to-have or need-to-know basis.

Those who are inclined to cause injury, damage, and theft or subordinate networks for their own purposes will do so with motivation and opportunity. Most will employ stealth or subterfuge, masking their identity to preclude accountability. Outsiders can pose the same accessibility risks by relying on process protection loopholes or social engineering to gain the unearned trust of gullible humans. They must penetrate the perimeters of facilities and networks to get to the valuable goods. True identity authentication for people, information, and goods in transit or at rest is required for large enterprises.

The most egregious attacks of our millennium were orchestrated by supposedly screened persons who penetrated protected environments with criminal intent. Identity credentials including security service badges and uniforms are often stolen by criminal groups to gain target access. Consider the attack in Luxor, Egypt, in 1997 that killed dozens of international tourists. The terrorists donned the color of authority by acquiring security uniforms to penetrate the site. By 2001,

---

[2]Bureau of Labor Statistics, "Workplace Violence Prevention 2005."
[3]Coenen, "True Cost of Fraud."
[4]ACFE, "2012 Global Fraud Study."

Al-Qaeda improved fraudulent identification acquisition from driver's licenses to passports to enable 9/11.[5]

How is one to trust an identity these days? A consumer survey performed by Javelin Strategy and Research found that in 2012, the rate of incidence for identity fraud in the United States increased for the second straight year: "Incidents of identity fraud affected 5.26 percent of U.S. adults [in 2012]" ... with "the total number of identity victims in 2012 [estimated at] 12.6 million."[6] Organized international crime rings harvest identities of the living and the dead for their own profit.

How many people with fraudulent credentials are already in our global institutions? Material employment application errors and omissions occurred at a rate of 46 percent in 2009, according to one study.[7] Organizational risk goes beyond the physical and fiscal injury imposed by a malefactor. It exposes the soft underbelly of organizational reputations, which are dearly dependent on all stakeholders believing that the institution recognized and mitigated all reasonable risk.

Assuming integrity once a credential is issued is not enough. Institutions must inspect what they expect. Governance must provide reoccurring audit measures and routinely assess accountability for acts and omissions that undermine security. Trusted agents including partners, associates, and service providers may be presumed to be legitimate only when they are routinely authenticated. Secure environments require additional multifactor controls to validate people, machines, manifests, passwords, and other credentials that permit routine access. In the words of Ronald Reagan, "Trust, but verify."[8]

3.2 LAYERED AND INTEGRATED SECURITY SOLUTIONS

In an article written for Utica College's *Journal of Economic Crime Management*, authors Norman Willox and Thomas Regan cite the research of UCLA Law Professor Lynn LoPucki in their discussion of

---

[5]National Commission on Terrorist Attacks in the United States, "The 9/11 Commission Report."

[6]Kirk, "Identity Fraud in the United States."

[7]Todd, "Workzone: Inquiries on Rise." According to Todd, "a 2009 study done by Roseland, N.J.-based data processing firm ADP showed that 46 percent of 5.5 million background checks revealed resume discrepancies, up from 45 percent the previous year and from 41 percent in 2007."

[8]Armstrong III, "Remember What Reagan Said about Trust."

identification systems that are presently at work in the private sector that may meet the requirements set forth in the Patriot Act:

> LoPucki provides three basic means for making identifications. The first such means is "knowledge-based" where persons are "recognized by demonstrating that they are in possession of information which only that person would be expected to know." The second basic means of human identification, according to LoPucki, is "token-based" identification, where a person is recognized by their possession of an item, such as a national identity card, or a driver's license, or a passport. Each of these "tokens" bears a description of the person that presumably would not match an imposter's person. The third means of human identification is "biometrics" which LoPucki states, quoting [Professor Roger] Clarke, refers to a "variety of identification techniques which are based on some physical and difficult-to-alienate characteristics." All three means of identification should be considered when devising an identity verification solution.[9]

There has been a great deal of conversation among asset protection professionals about the convergence of physical (people, buildings, and assets) and logical (computers, networks, and information) protection. True security convergence is a bit elusive given the complexity of integrating diverse systems and processes.

Networks include human transportation, data, and cargo pathways. All are prerequisites for cultural and commercial viability and growth. Access control must enable trusted agents while denying malefactors, like a semipermeable membrane allowing nutrients to penetrate a cell while barring toxins.

Layered and integrated security, including access control, can mitigate risk to physical and logical spaces by recognizing and challenging potentially destructive agents on the perimeter and denying access. People, process, and technology together provide solutions. Knowledge-based authentication, coordinated with policy controls and exception reporting, can link physical security with logical infrastructure in sophisticated environments. Consider the integrated approach in Figure 3.2.

---

[9]Willox and Regan, "Identity Fraud," 8.

Layered Security and Analytics Support Mission

- **Accountability assurance** (Audit, Correct, Measure)
- **Response, reporting and notification** (Compliance exceptions, QA, Safety, Security)
  (Conveyance, data, machine, person, manifest, SKU, transaction, and vehicle integrity)
- **Multi-factor authentication**
- **Risk-driven security, safety, and QA policy or standards**
- **All hazards awareness, training, communications**

Mission: Protect people. Secure assets. Contribute profitably.

Figure 3.2 Layered Security Approach. © Crime Prevention Associates. All rights reserved.

Beginning with the baseline objective or goal, our prioritized risk awareness can be adapted to relevant policy and standards that rely on multiple-factor authentication, exception reporting, and response for measured security assurance. There is little argument that we live in a risk-rich environment evidenced by daily reports of natural and man-made events that injure, damage, and disrupt. Compensatory common denominator mitigation is required for emergency preparedness. Otherwise people, assets, critical processes, products, and services will be subject to ongoing injury and disruption without relief.

Good security practices must extend to partnerships throughout a global enterprise. Witness the quality assurance and brand reputation issues that have been introduced by suppliers in recent years. Integrated standards and processes protect the enterprise. Laissez faire attitudes to extended partner security can be an Achilles' heel for relatively secure organizations.

Figure 3.3 graphically illustrates 2009 country threat levels for stakeholders who must calculate risk for a certain region. FrontierMEDEX color ratings are as follows: red is very high, orange is high, yellow is medium, green is low, and blue is very low.

Figure 3.4 is a presumption of risk exercise for a food supply chain. Using risk intelligence data, FrontierMEDEX categorized countries by security threat level for mitigation considerations. Finite dollars for Authorized Economic Operator (AEO, World Customs Organization), C-TPAT (US Customs Trade Partnership against Terrorism), Food Defense, or ISO supply chain security standard compliance will more than likely be directed at prioritized trade routes based on risk.

World class medical, safety and security solutions.
www.frontiermedex.com

SECURITY THREAT LEVELS

Country	Rating	Country	Rating	Country	Rating	Country	Rating	Country	Rating	Country	Rating
Afghanistan	5: CfGIKPTW	China	2: cdefgt	Haiti	4: CDGKp	Mauritius	2: c	Saudi Arabia	3: dOpt	Uruguay	2: cdg
Albania	3: cdG	Colombia	4: CDgIKt	Honduras	4: CDGKp	Mexico	4: CdGK	Senegal	3: cDgi	U.S. Virgin Islands	3: c
Algeria	4: cDKpT	Comoros	3:	Hungary	2: Cd	Micronesia	1:	Serbia	2: Cdf0	Uzbekistan	4: cEGt
Angola	4: CdG	Congo (DRC)	5: CDFGIK	Iceland	1: d	Moldova	3: Cdds	Seychelles	1:	Vanuatu	1: b
Argentina	2: CDgk	Congo (RoC)	4: CdFGt	India	3: CDeFGlpsT	Monaco	2:	Sierra Leone	4: CdOps	Venezuela	4: CDGKpt
Armenia	3: cdgw	Costa Rica	2: cd	Indonesia	4: CDfPsT	Mongolia	2: C	Singapore	2:	Vietnam	3: ce
Aruba	2:	Cote d'Ivoire	5: CDfGP	Iran	3: cdGPt	Montenegro	2: cds	Slovakia	2: c	Yemen	5: DGkPSTW
Australia	2: cd	Croatia	2: cdg	Ireland	2: cd	Morocco	3: Cdt	Slovenia	2: c	Zambia	3: Cdg
Austria	2: cd	Cuba	3: cd	Israel	4: dpT	Mozambique	3: Cdgkp	Solomon Isles	3: cfgP	Zimbabwe	4: CdGPV
Azerbaijan	3: cDfw	Cyprus	2: cp	Italy	2: Cdt	Myanmar	4: caFlpt	Somalia	5: CGfGkPTW	**Country Threat Level**	
Bahamas	2: C	Czech Republic	2: cd	Jamaica	4: CdG	Namibia	3: c	South Africa	4: CDg	1 – Very Low	
Bahrain	3: DPSt	Denmark	2: Cd	Japan	2: c	Nepal	3: CDgkPtV	South Korea	2: cO	2 – Low Threat	
Bangladesh	4: CDGPt	Djibouti	3: CD	Jordan	3: DPt	Netherlands	2: cdt	South Sudan	5: CDFGfGPW	3 – Medium Threat	
Barbados	1: c	Dom. Republic	3: CDG	Kazakhstan	3: ceGt	New Caledonia	2: d	Spain	2: CDt	4 – High Threat	
Belarus	3: CdEGP	Dominica	2:	Kenya	4: CdFGkPTV	New Zealand	1:	Sri Lanka	3: dfiPt	5 – Very High Threat	
Belgium	2: CD	Ecuador	2: Cdgk	Kosovo	4: CdfP	Nicaragua	3: CdGp	Sudan	5: CDFGkPW	**Country Threats**	
Belize	3: Cg	Egypt	4: CDGPt	Kuwait	3: dgFt	Niger	4: CfGlkPT	Suriname	3: Cdf0	C: Crime	
Benin	3: CG	El Salvador	4: Cdgk	Kyrgyzstan	4: CDfGPt	Nigeria	5: CDFGkPST	Swaziland	3: CdgP	D: Demonstrations / Protests	
Bermuda	1:	Eq. Guinea	3: cG	Laos	3: Cei	North Korea	3: EOp	Sweden	2: Cd	E: Espionage	
Bhutan	2: ti	Eritrea	4: CP	Latvia	2: cg	Norway	2: cdt	Switzerland	2: c	F: Ethnic Conflict	
Bolivia	3: cDGkP	Estonia	2: E	Lebanon	4: CDGkPST	Oman	2: d	Syria	5: CDGkPSTW	G: Graft / Corruption	
Bosnia & Herz.	3: cdFGP	Ethiopia	3: cIpt	Lesotho	3: Cdp	Pakistan	5: CDGkPST	Taiwan	2: c	I: Insurgency	
Botswana	2: Cd	Fiji	3: cp	Lesser Antilles	2: cd	Palestinian Ter.	5: cDkPT	Tajikistan	4: CDpt	K: Kidnapping	
Brazil	3: Cdgk	Finland	2: Cd	Liberia	4: CdGps	Panama	3: Cdgk	Tanzania	3: CdGpst	P: Political Stability	
British Virgin Isl.	1: c	France	2: CDt	Libya	5: cDFGkPBT	Papua N. Guinea	4: CDfPV	Thailand	3: cdipt	S: Sectarian Conflict	
Brunei	2: c	French Guiana	2: cd	Lithuania	2: c	Paraguay	3: Cd0lk	Timor Leste	4: Cdfgp	T: Terrorism	
Bulgaria	3: cdGk	Gabon	3: Cdg	Luxembourg	2: c	Peru	3: COgld	Togo	4: cdGP	V: Elections	
Burkina Faso	3: CdGk	Gambia	3: cO	Macedonia	3: cdFG	Philippines	4: CD9kpT	Tonga	2: cd	W: War	
Burundi	4: CdgIPt	Georgia	4: cdt	Madagascar	3: CDgPv	Poland	2: Cd	Trin. & Tob.	3: CdG	Note: Lower-case letter ratings	
C.A. Republic	5: CDGKP	Germany	2: CDt	Malawi	3: cdg	Portugal	2: cd	Tunisia	3: DkPt	signify that threat is significant, but to	
Cambodia	3: CeG	Ghana	3: Cdg	Malaysia	3: Dfstv	Puerto Rico	3: Cd	Turkey	3: cdiT	a lesser extent or a regional issue.	
Cameroon	3: CDGk	Greece	2: CDt	Maldives	2: ccp	Qatar	2: pt	Turkmenistan	3: cEO	Note: Health-related issues are	
Canada	2: cd	Greenland	1:	Mali	4: CdGkPT	Romania	2: ccp	U.A.E.	2: pt	endemic throughout much of Africa.	
Cape Verde	2: c	Guatemala	4: CdGK	Malta	2: c	Russia	3: CdeGkfT	Uganda	4: CdfGk		
Cayman Islands	1: C	Guinea	4: CDGP	Marshall Isles	1:	Rwanda	4: CIl	Ukraine	3: CdGk		
Chad	5: CdFGlPt	Guinea Bissau	4: CdGP	Mauritania	4: GkpT	Samoa	1: c	United Kingdom	2: Cdst		
Chile	2: CDgt	Guyana	3: Cdfg			SaoTome & Principe	3: d	United States	2: Cdt		

Figure 3.3 Security Threat Levels. © 2013 FrontierMEDEX Inc. All rights reserved. Used with permission.

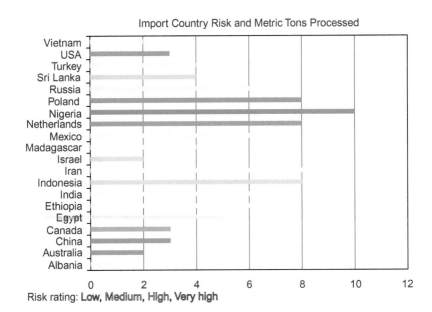

Figure 3.4 Import Country Risk. © Crime Prevention Associates. All rights reserved.

Risk presumptions illustrated in gradient colors with percent tonnage imported allows stakeholders to absorb the main mitigation opportunities. Nigeria in this instance stands out for both the highest risk (red) and the largest raw product contributor per metric ton (10). Prioritizing the Nigerian supply chain for risk mitigation including contingency identification of other procurement sources would be likely in this exercise scenario.

Combinations of manmade and natural hazards together with business dependency for high quality product volume often help make the supply chain protection decisions. Priority election for AEO, C-TPAT, or ISO security compliance requires risk intelligence and complementary mitigations. Identity authentication for people, data, and cargo is a primary defense. Consider a supply chain model (Figure 3.5) that protects from the farm at origin to the consumer's plate.

Beginning at the top right and moving down, country origin risk information is supplemented with product quality assurance requirements to ensure delivery of goods to the market place. Product inspections, sampling, and testing are likely to occur at various intervals

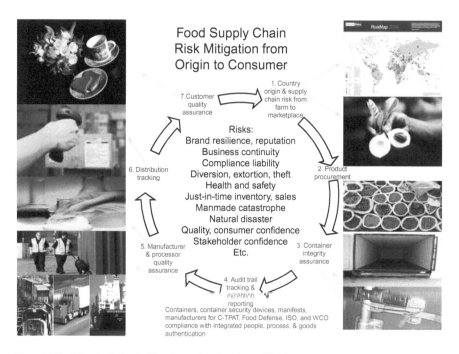

Figure 3.5 Food Supply Chain. © Crime Prevention Associates. All rights reserved.

along the path. Personnel, container, and logistics integrity help ensure protection against the elements and unauthorized agents who may adulterate, steal, or convert drayage to their own criminal enterprise. Timely exception detection and reporting by suppliers, drayage companies, manufacturers, and government agencies can mitigate a host of health and security concerns. Toxicological assays and warehouse management distribution systems assure manufactured product safety and recall facilitation. Most importantly, auditable tracking and quality assurance inspection of raw materials from origin to manufacture and the subsequent safe delivery to the consumer enables confidence in global trade.

Starbucks undertook similar measures and precautions including testing GE CommerceGuard container security devices (CSDs) in 2006.[10] CSD-equipped containers wirelessly communicate with readers at authorized packing, port, and manufacturing facilities remitting container access history. When layered with handheld or fixed enabling devices and video or audio authentication peripherals and other security devices, legitimate access to protected cargo and exception detection was assured. The layered, networked security approach for suppliers, trade cooperatives, customs, and the supply chain owner met or exceeded US Customs-Trade Partnership Against Terrorism (C-TPAT), ISO supply chain guidelines, and US Food and Drug Administration (FDA) Food Defense practices.

Unfortunately, the GE CommerceGuard innovation was abandoned in 2009 due to inadequate market adoption, but not before it was validated as a virtual permission access enabling a security audit trail for timely detection of security and quality assurance issues. Importantly, it achieved these objectives cost-effectively at less than $35 per container. Pilot introductions also informed other affordable conveyance integrity assurance methodology.

Networked security environments that may be successfully attacked in the future must be built to perform as stand-alone systems. Evolving integrated security approaches in developing countries is instructive for maintaining security even in challenging communications environments. Maintaining redundant and stand-alone capabilities for network capable peripherals are contingencies to be considered.

---

[10]D'Addario, "ISO/PAS 28001 Enables Starbucks Coffee Company's Supply Chain Strategy."

3.3 INSPECT WHO YOU EXPECT

Trusted agent authentication cannot be overemphasized. Detection of unauthorized use is germane when legitimate networks can be converted by criminals and terrorists for an unintended agenda.

The terrorists of 9/11 were not readily identifiable criminals. Their identity frauds were detectable and they should have drawn attention with their exceptional behavior. Both risk detection and security mitigation should require at least two-factor authentication of the identity or privileged activity. Finite resources require us to triage exceptions based on accepted rules of risk and intelligence.

The tragedy of 9/11 was not the first nor will it be the last fatal lapse of security. Recall the security blunder of the Trojans in missing the Greek threat at Troy. The Trojan horse metaphor from the thirteenth century BC epic tale lives on in modern logical system attacks, where detrimental data packets with destructive agendas deceptively insinuate themselves in computer networks.

Two- and three-factor authentications may be required for effective people, data, and cargo protection in future secure communities. Smart technology capabilities may ensure that the person, machine, and activity are acting in accordance with acceptable use standards. For instance, integrated identity authentication may associate a trusted biometric for a person against a unique vehicle transponder and an encoded manifest for the cargo.

These capabilities may allow interdiction of high risk cargo from accidental distribution of tainted food to purposeful delivery for weapons of mass destruction. Such integration will differentiate legitimate transactions from prohibited ones. Will the truck pulling up to your building be a legitimate delivery or another Timothy McVeigh? The American terrorist blew up the federal building in Oklahoma City in 1995 with a homemade weapon of mass destruction delivered by a relatively innocuous Ryder truck, commonly leased for deliveries. Do the converged cargo and driver identification credentials match the manifest or has the supply chain been compromised? Do access barriers effectively isolate a threat on the outside of the perimeter?

Protection compliance professionals and communities that care continuously improve layered security if they are able. Six Sigma performance, with less than 3.4 misses in one million transactions, is the high bar for quality assurance.[11] Most of us are a long way off from that level; but that does not preclude our commitment to testing potential security solutions for incremental continuous improvement. Human intelligence, imagination, risk awareness, access credentials, and systems integration will enable just-in-time exceptional risk detection and mitigation. Organizations that effectively learn from their own mistakes and those of others will marginalize the risks that threaten their sustainability.

Discussion Exercise

Describe your access control policy and standards. Illustrate any gaps for true identity authentication as part of your employment or contracting practices. Do you require it as a condition for new hires and contract assignments requiring physical or network access? Are applicant and contractor identity and reputation diligence mandated? Is exception reporting required through your supply chain to preclude or mitigate potential for charges of negligence or inadequate security?

Additional Information and Resources

1. "ISO IEC 27002: 2005 Information Security Standard: Translated into Plain English," Praxiom Research Group Limited: http://www.praxiom.com/iso-17799-2005.htm.
2. Transit Security Design Considerations, Chapter 5.0: Access Management, US Department of Transportation, Federal Transit Administration: http://www.fta.dot.gov/safetysecurity/12537_12972.html.
3. World Customs Organization SAFE Framework of Standards: http://www.wcoomd.org/en/topics/facilitation/instrument-and-tools/tools/safe_package.aspx.
4. ISO 28000:2007 – Specification for Security Management Systems for the Supply Chain: http://www.iso.org/iso/home/store/catalogue_tc/catalogue_detail.htm?csnumber = 44641.
5. National Geographic's Illicit: The Dark Trade: http://www.pbs.org/illicit/.

●●●

... R.H. and her attorney mounted a compulsive shopper defense that failed to win her freedom. It effectively reduced a potential seven-year sentence to four. She served one. "[R.H.] was released from prison in

---

[11]Walshe, Harvey, and Jas, *Connecting Knowledge and Performance*, 175.

January 2004 after completing her sentence for embezzling $3.7 million from her employer. But [R.H.] still owes more than $2 million in restitution and has not had her voting rights restored ... Reached at her new workplace, a manufacturing firm in Port Orchard, she declined to comment."[12]

---

[12]*Seattle Times,* "Scores of Felons Voted Illegally."

CHAPTER 4

Prioritizing Risk Mitigation

Connecting risk priorities to effective security mitigation improvement is helped by demonstrating return-on-investment (ROI)-capable security solutions and protection quality assurance. Risk frequency and severity must be persuasively mitigated or reduced to enable mission with improved stakeholder confidence. Piloting innovations like "interactive security" (featuring video- and audio-monitored event confirmation) are detailed in this chapter.

●●●

It is still dark as Washington awakens from the three-day Fourth of July weekend: 5:15 a.m. on Monday, July 7, 1997. The day-shift supervisor arrives to begin the new week at the Starbucks on Wisconsin Avenue in Georgetown. In the parking lot, she sees the Saturn coupe belonging to the night-shift supervisor, Caity Mahoney. This is odd; Caity should have closed up at 8 the night before. The day supervisor unlocks the door, steps inside. The lights are on. Music is playing. A rag and cleaning fluid are out. A broom and dustpan slant against a booth. On the counter is a work schedule and a muffin, unwrapped. Farther on, in a back room and hallway, she finds them. Mary Caitrin Mahoney, 16 days short of her 25th birthday. Emory Allen Evans, 25. Aaron David Goodrich, 18. She runs out into the street and flags down a bus. The driver calls 911.[1]

Starbucks rallied around the victims' families immediately. Howard Schultz contacted each to commiserate with them on their loss. He pledged that the remodeled store would be reopened as a "living memorial" with all future net profits from the Georgetown store to be contributed to "keep their spirits alive."[2]

The cross-functional task force correctly anticipated needs including grief counselors, benefits coordinators, a transparent security inquiry, and safety review. The case drew national and international attention. The dearth of forensic evidence (no suspect DNA, weapon, or fingerprints) and the absence of eyewitnesses set the stage for a protracted

[1]Leen, "A Dance with Death."
[2]Hansen, "Starbucks to Reopen."

investigation. The crime scene was inspected and video taped upon release by the DC homicide team. Security components, including alarms and the safe, were in working order. The $100,000 reward offer and other resources were made available to Trainum and Garrett to expedite their investigation.

4.1 PRIORITIZING PREVENTION

Starbucks was, at the time of the Georgetown homicides, arguably the least robbed "quick service" food and beverage entity of its size in North America. Nevertheless the situational opportunity for improved security programming was clear. An unsolved murder brought more questions than answers. Anxiety for personnel and customer safety drove unanimous support for prioritizing any proven improvement. "Proven" is the key word. The presumption that any prevention investment is automatic is more often than not wrong. Even the wealthiest corporation must approve and prioritize investments based on qualified benefit.

Choices are made in context. Hazard frequency and severity are rankable. Robbery risk is clear for US cash-handling businesses following significant research. Other security needs, including better background screening and employment diligence, had to compete with access control upgrades for Y2K network concerns; supply chain, store, and information security improvements; exception fraud detection; and the development of compliance and investigative resources to support the core business needs. Finite resources were available for all security improvements.

It is important to distinguish the value of prevention and mitigation spending that incrementally ensures return on investment by either loss prevention or suppression. The accountability and arrest of a serial offender, for instance, tends to ensure frequency reduction. The certainty of accountability can have a chilling effect on both criminal activity or acts and omissions contrary to prudent prevention policy practices.

The behavior of both the would-be criminal and the community member who engages in high-risk acts or omissions undermining security may be modified. Dedicated surveillance integrated with barriers and response capability has been known to effectively influence the predilection of fraudsters, robbers, and even suicide bombers from their primary targets, because the combination of obstruction and nimble response can deny the objective. Similarly, policy violators will adopt acceptable behavior when the risk of detection and sanctions for unapproved behavior are high.

To leverage events and prioritize risks with layered prevention, exception detection, and mitigation response, we will consider "preventioneering." The term appears to have been adopted in Texas by a group that was relied on for fighting oil well fires and is now a segment of Halliburton. The term refers to the "non-critical response efforts on pre-event and preventative services [of Boots & Coots], such as site inspections, contingency planning and training."[3]

For our purposes, preventioneering applies to the art of leveraging injury and damage events to influence adoption of proven sustainable prevention and mitigation. We also credit Walt Disney's "Imagineering" here to emphasize that our communities need thoughtful imagination and innovation.[4] As noted in Chapter Three, integrated layers that promote safety and security while advancing the community mission require thoughtful planning.

4.2 PILOTING NEW SECURITY

Preventioneering presumes that proven mitigation may be engineered and implemented for enduring protection across an enterprise before risk events occur. Pilot studies are one means to economically proof a concept or business case for risk impact, cost, and benefit. Measured results from pilots influence wider implementation or additional research.

In the wake of the Georgetown homicides, Starbucks vowed to test and implement any approach that reasonably made people safer. Interactive security was prioritized as a potential solution to commercial armed robbery risk. Starbucks had the lowest reported victimization rate for similarly sized quick service organizations in 1997. Most quick service chains were reporting 80 or more robberies per 1,000 units in that period. Convenience store chains commonly reported

---

[3]Rigzone, "Boots and Coots."
[4]For more background on Walt Disney Imagineering, see: http://wdi.disneycareers.com/en/default/.

more than 120 per 1,000 units. The potential for continuous improvement drove additional innovation.

Successful robbery prevention and suppression pilots incorporate elements of Crime Prevention through Environmental Design (CPTED). Natural surveillance with unobstructed windows, good lighting, and clear lines of vision can be supplemented with digital video and alarm components that confirm crimes in progress. The addition of "smart safe" time-delay and time-lock technology hinders the availability of the primary objective: cash. The so-called "interactive security" capability enables crime victims to discreetly trigger emergency duress alarms (i.e., a robbery in progress) for security monitoring agents to see, hear, and report to authorities.

The project innovatively combined proven prevention engineering with new applications. The CPTED principle of natural surveillance brought cash handling and the safe out of the back room. The concept was proven at the Southland Corporation (operating as 7-Eleven stores) in the late 1970s.[5] Moving "smart safes" from the back room combined with clearing windows of signage enabled police and passers by to witness cash handling with the effect of putting would-be robbers on stage for later identification.

The Southland security team piloted an earlier version of interactive security combining alarms and cameras for suspect identification and apprehension. In the early 1980s Polaroid instant cameras in a sound-proof housing were tested at 7-Eleven Stores in Columbus, Ohio, and New Orleans, Louisiana. Wireless bill clips signaled the cameras for a series of instant photos when criminals demanded or stripped all the money from the till. The concept improved at Long John Silver's, demonstrating return on investment using a duress dial on a mechanical time-delay safe with 35 mm bank hold-up cameras in Houston, Texas.[6] The operator only had to add ten to his or her combination while opening the safe to trigger the camera and a silent alarm monitored by a central station.

The Southland robbery violence prevention programming emanated from research with convicted robbers who rated the attractiveness of potential commercial targets.[7] Subsequent to the development of risk

---

[5]D'Addario, *Loss Prevention through Crime Analysis.*
[6]Ibid., 70.
[7]Crow and Bull, *Robbery Deterrence.*

Table 4.1 Target Attractiveness Ranking by Adult and Juvenile Robbers

Factors	Adults Robbers Rank Order*	Juvenile Robbers Rank Order*
What would be important to you if you were to rob a convenience store?		
1. Escape route	1	1
2. Amount of money	2	2
3. Active police patrols	5	3
4. Anonymity	3	4
5. Armed guards	4	5
6. Armed clerks	6	6
7. Number of clerks	9	7
8. Interference	7	8
9. Bullet resistant barriers	8	9
10. Alarm systems	10	10
11. Number of customers	11	11
12. Camera system	12	12
13. Video recording	13	13
14. Unarmed guards	14	14

Scale: 1 = most important; 14 = least important.

awareness and mitigation measures, a more than 90 percent drop in the robbery homicide rate followed companywide implementation. Research by Dr. Rosemary Erickson of the Athena Research Corporation has proven that the amount of ready cash is a primary attraction for robbers.[8] Erickson, a forensic sociologist, security consultant, and expert witness, surveyed adult convicts in the 1970s, 80s, and 90s as well as juvenile robbers in 2001 to determine rankings for selecting robbery targets. See Table 4.1 for Erickson's robbery target attractiveness ranking by adult and juvenile offenders.

Erickson's research and ranking data proves the value of barriers and cash control but should not dissuade the use of cameras. After all, anonymity is the fourth-ranked concern for robbers. Integrated and layered systems deprive robbers of anonymity, particularly when lighting and natural visibility enable police or passers by to detect or witness a crime in progress and camera placement documents suspects in the act or positively identifies those responsible after the fact. Similarly, audio enables monitoring agents to dispatch law enforcement with certainty even when cameras

[8]Erickson, *Teenage Robbers*, 7.

are disabled. Both make possible higher rates of identification leading to apprehension and incarceration. Reduced crime rates follow once serial offenders are removed from the scene. Transparent communication of identification certainty will alter the target election of many.

The interactive security concept evolved at Hardees Food Systems with the integration of video cameras and smart safes that enabled digital access control, time delay, and discreet duress alarm in the Philadelphia Roy Rogers restaurants in 1993. Mike Arrighi, corporate loss prevention manager, reported an 83 percent reduction in reported crimes. The $34,000 per year net sales performance and estimated 400 percent return on security investment from the Philadelphia pilot paved the way for enterprise adoption for all new restaurants in 1994.[9]

4.3 INTEGRATION

Camera and audio input integration is an opportunity for alarm panel transmission to a monitoring facility. Event corroboration for police notification offers a pathway for false alarm prevention. Two-way communications enable monitoring agents to see and hear their clients. Smart safes with time-delay and time-lock features allow deterrent cash control. Virtual alarm reporting and cash control deny criminals cash, anonymity, and escape options.

The integration of CPTED processes and technology can either dissuade robbers from their target or aid in their apprehension after the fact. The presence of cameras and signage effectively communicate improved capabilities to deter other crimes and increase safety. The perception of improved security at point of sale has chilling effects on robbery, fraud, and theft including shoplifting while improving accountability. Objective performance metrics include event incidence, loss cost, sales, cash over/short, and inventory shrinkage. Audio with alarm events assist monitoring personnel for event corroboration when camera views are compromised.

There is always some risk in testing new process and technology. Influential operators that have "been there, done that" are more than willing to share their disappointments with past security experience including lack of results and unexpected expense for monitoring,

[9]D'Addario, *Manager's Violence Survival Guide*, 62.

maintenance, false alarms, or other missteps. Piloting new security solutions may be viewed anxiously as pioneering out of the core skill area. Operators seem to prefer "fast follower" status for proven solutions. Engaging operations management experience and recommendations before, during, and after a pilot is essential to managing expectations and outcomes. Address stakeholder concerns and incorporate them into your plan.

Data supporting the efficacy of any security practice is also essential when piloting new concepts. For instance, simply moving cash security up front from a back office and introducing time delay to reduce armed robbery violence is not likely to be well received without illuminating conversation and training. Moving the cash closer to the customer may seem counter intuitive to what retailers traditionally feel are good practices. Hiding the safe in the back and providing cash unhindered by technology during a robbery may feel safe to business operators despite more than 30 years of research that contradicts these opinions. Conversation and communications tend to correct misinformation that may hold back a project.

4.4 GALVANIZING RESOURCES

Any large capital investment requires cross-functional support. Security does not get a free ride from a rigorous capital review process. Projects may be chartered and presented to a diverse committee of executives representing many parts of the business. Transparency of risks and benefits is only part of the dialogue. Setting the clear expectation that interactive security reduces the frequency of the risk but doesn't eliminate it is the job of the protection professional.

Hazards including robbery violence cannot be totally eliminated. The likelihood of having a violent episode during a pilot was not unforeseeable. Leveraging the benefits of improved safety for engagement, supervised deliveries, and elimination of videotape maintenance are tangible extras that appeal enterprise-wide to human resources, legal, retail, supply chain, and other stakeholders.

Questions will be asked and answered prior to approval of funds for implementation: How will the pilot affect the culture or brand perception? Will cameras or audio have a chilling effect on personnel and customers who might presume that Big Brother is watching or listening? Could potential negative customer perception impact sales and profit? Does an expectation of privacy mean that audio may be used for alarm events only? How does the project rank with competing requests for return on investment?

Pilot stores are ideally selected with operations input. Data will guide but operators ultimately own the risk. Other departments may assist. Marketing, for instance, can inform control store selection. Control stores will ideally match demographics including neighborhood, sales, and physical footprint. Test and control unit selection across broad geography in multiple markets can add relevance for test results.

Surveys can identify interested sponsors and candidate test locations. "What store comes to mind as a likely candidate for a security problem?" Survey experts may also use pre installation and post-installation questionnaires to measure pre test and post test security attitudes or confidence.

Good practices should link strategic and operational objectives (see Figure 4.1). Training and audit can play key roles in any change management process. Frequently asked questions and answers facilitate technology and process introductions.

Pilot security performance informs prevention and mitigation standards adoption. Total cost of ownership elements may include facilities

Retail Interactive Security Good Practice Objectives

Strategic

- Improve customer, employee, and invitee safety with supervised access control, cash & inventory handling, and risk response
- Improve profitability with crime deterrence and accountability via digital video and audio alarm event or exception confirmation for assault, burglary, embezzlement, fraud, robbery, theft, etc.
- Comply with workplace violence avoidance best practices

Operational

- Enable cash availability for speedier customer service with compensating 'smart safe' security features including: time-delay, time-lock, audit, and discreet duress
- Enable exception investigations, merchandising decisions, and staffing efficiencies with combined video and exception reporting analytic capability
- Facilitate same day bank revenue credit when networked with approved cash couriers

Figure 4.1 Retail Good Practice Objectives. © Crime Prevention Associates. All rights reserved.

renovation, new hardware introductions, network integration, capital investment, maintenance expenses, and training.

Research data including the likelihood of violence with unmonitored safe operations and customer service efficiency can garner operational support for cash handling monitoring and safe relocation on the sales floor. Operators can be encouraged to explain to customers (to balance privacy concerns) that cameras and audio are limited to exceptional events in the most public areas only. Camera views may be deferred away from café seating areas where privacy may be more expected.

Signage should be considered to transparently communicate risk mitigation and assist operators in alleviating concerns that might arise. "For Our Protection" messaging may simultaneously inform criminals, customers, employees, service providers, and visitors, as shown in Figure 4.2. Training including frequently asked questions enables operators to be conversant with program objectives and communication opportunities.

4.5 DOCUMENTING PILOT RESULTS

Commercial armed robbery test store and control store results were documented at Southland, Jerrico, Hardees, and Starbucks throughout the 1980s and 1990s. Robberies, burglaries, and cash and inventory losses for interactive security stores were significantly less than control stores. Event frequency suppression was persuasively evidenced in each instance

Figure 4.2 For Our Protection Sign. © Diebold, Inc. All rights reserved. Used with permission.

with significant ROI. Incremental sales and net profits of the test stores outperforming control stores influenced innovation adoptions. Test pilots influenced change management, including construction design guidelines, to accommodate both new construction and remodel designs.

Starbucks pilot results were similar to those posted by Hardees Food Systems for its Philadelphia 1993 Roy Rogers test. Results recognized at the 1994 University of Edmonton and American Society for Industrial Security's Profit Centre II conference included an 84 percent crime reduction and $34,000 net revenue increase.

Technology innovation and implementation can be compared to playing an accordion. Both bring discovery of unanticipated notes. Unintended consequences require practical adjustments. Retrofitting point-of-sale counter space was one clear opportunity for improvement. Retrofit installations were scheduled for night hours to minimally disrupt operations.

Eliminating videotape rotation and introducing personal computer-based digital imaging was initially a big win for operations. The introduction of network capable security equipment in a dial-up environment was not ideal. Although it successfully influenced criminal behavior and achieved business results, the solution was technically disappointing. Image delivery to central station alarm monitoring was initially hampered by reboot issues. Video transmission followed audio too slowly at intervals of up to two minutes.

Device standards were changed and improved with every performance shortfall thanks to the diligence of the Retail P&AP, Information Technology, and service providers. Red phones that were initially tested to report high risk situations were eliminated due to the difficulty of integration with video and associated false alarm frequency. Cost savings were realized with improved security equipment expense for cameras, digital video recorders, and smart safes.

Benefits outweighed difficulties. The network environment for virtual monitoring has caught up to eliminate dial-up dependency for additional savings. Retail finance analysts corroborated that test store retrofits outperformed non interactive stores for incremental sales on an annual basis.

After 9/11 it was comforting to know that interactive security could be leveraged for protection beyond commercial armed robbery violence. Risk adjacency to numerous potential high value terrorist targets offered the prospect of greater community protection. There were more hazards afoot than just potential armed robbers.

By 2007, capability to integrate exception detection with digital video and audio confirmation capability was proven. Networked digital photography could remind retail and critical facilities stakeholders that security connectivity was working for both protection and exception documentation. Holiday greetings combined with risk reporting could recommunicate the culture of care.

The certainty that crimes are discoverable in real time in a networked environment influences many choices. The case was made that the priority risk of armed robbery violence could be mitigated while improving other business outcomes. Events and data had informed security solution decisions. The results influenced community confidence and funding for additional risk mitigations. The cross-functional teams had evolved to proactive ROI-capable people and asset risk mitigation rather than relying on their ability to react after the fact. They demonstrated capability to assess and prioritize risk, design and implement mitigation, galvanize resources, measure improvements, and ensure accountability.

Discussion Exercise

Describe a priority security practice for your community that resulted from a pilot study. Identify any events that influenced your security solution. Describe your approach to communicating the risks, benefits, and measures that made the persuasive case for resource allocation.

Additional Information and Resources

1. Oscar Newman, Defensible Space: *Crime Prevention through Urban Design* (New York: Macmillan, 1972): http://www.ncjrs.gov/App/Publications/abstract.aspx?ID = 9697.
2. Timothy D. Crowe, Lawrence Fennelly, *Crime Prevention through Environmental Design* (Butterworth-Heinemann, 2013): http://store.elsevier.com/product.jsp?isbn = 9780124116351.
3. George K. Campbell, *Measures and Metrics in Corporate Security* (Security Executive Council, 2006): https://www.securityexecutivecouncil.com/secstore/index.php?main_page = product_info&products_id = 324.

●●●———————————————————————————————

... [Starbucks] has chosen the Community Foundation for the National Capital Region, an organization that makes grants to non-profit groups, to receive all the profits from the Georgetown store for as long as the store is open. The foundation will distribute the money to anti-violence groups. [In 2008], starting with a $25,000 check ... the store's profits [began to] go to Circle of Hope, a foundation initiative that works with youths in three high-crime DC neighborhoods.[10]

In 2000, Carl Cooper pleaded guilty to the Georgetown murders and is presently serving consecutive life sentences without the possibility of parole in a US federal penitentiary.

[10]Paulson, "Starbucks Moves beyond Tragedy."

CHAPTER 5

Estimating Return on Security Investment

Risk and mitigation both feature a total cost of ownership. Protection practitioners, who soberly and accurately calculate the comprehensive liability of unmitigated hazards as well as the benefits of effective risk mitigation, are best prepared for influencing policy, standards, practices, program development, and community outcomes. Charting the course to mitigate emerging risk provides a means to show the "big picture" and to influence cross-functional support and investment. Security will not get a "free ride" from organizational expectations that include effective risk mitigation, operating on or below plan and meeting or exceeding expectations.

Risk events that could recur drive enterprise action. Heidi Parr, a Starbucks investigator, coordinated an investigation into an identity and bank fraud scheme that began with a former Starbucks employee with three banks and the FBI. At first the bank frauds appeared to be coincidental, with identity theft unrelated to the workplace. Seattle was one of the cities reporting the highest rates for identity theft in the United States at the time. Early fraud reports did not exceed the victimization rate for King County. That assessment changed as the number of victims reporting similar losses rose as bank notifications of overdrawn accounts arrived. Appearances indicated that it was an insider's work.

The investigators looked for a common denominator between Starbucks and the three banks. Photographs of branch bank check cashers using fraudulent identification and posing as Starbucks personnel were distributed regionally with a reward for information resulting in arrests and convictions. Detailed information regarding the crime methodology was provided, but bank processing errors delayed discontinuation of the criminal enterprise. Payroll file transmission was analyzed for security robustness. All persons with human resource data access to victim records were surveyed using an investigative questionnaire.

Additional countermeasures included reducing data access, introducing encryption, and protecting identities of the victims. The cross-functional team of P&AP, Information Technology, Law and Corporate Affairs, Human Resources, and Global Communications ensured the success of efforts to stem further damage and comply with stakeholder expectations.

In interviews pursuant to an arrest, the FBI developed a person of interest that Starbucks P&AP personnel corroborated as having access. The indictment news of April 2005 came approximately 17 months after the first reported victim detailed his experience. Thousands were apprised of the breach, investigative status, and compensatory identity protection measures.

The issues of the case were potentially larger than an interstate criminal enterprise. The potential global data security implications for partners and stakeholders were significant. Although customer data was segregated and protected, any insinuation that it could be at risk might undermine consumer confidence in the brand.

Timely mitigation and compensatory security actions must be demonstrated with any breach. Recent consumer reaction pursuant to one multinational criminal conspiracy proves the point. Eleven international players were indicted or arrested for harvesting, transmitting, and fraudulently using more than 40 million customer credit accounts from US retailers. Accounts "sniffed" at nine US retailers were dumped to overseas servers. "Officials with the Department of Justice said the people indicted were part of a criminal ring that stretched from the United States to Eastern Europe and East Asia, highlighting the global nature of computer crime. Charges of conspiracy, computer intrusion, fraud, and identity theft have been brought against people from Estonia, Ukraine, China, and Belarus, as well as the United States."[1]

TJ Maxx was one of three companies that settled with the US Federal Trade Commission (FTC) on charges that it "failed to provide reasonable and appropriate security for sensitive consumer information" by agreeing to extensive audits. The FTC was not able to impose financial penalties for the data breach. It has been requesting this power from Congress since 2005 to no avail.[2]

---

[1] Baribeau and Nakashima, "11 Charged in Global Theft."
[2] Cateriniccia, "Companies Avoid Financial Penalties."

Stakeholders require responsible organizations to react to loss events in a persuasive manner in order to preclude their recurrence. Unanticipated events sometimes afford the benefit of the doubt. Repeated loss incidents are subject to charges of negligence, gross negligence, or criminal negligence and may carry penalties or subvert insurance coverage.

5.1 CHARTING A COURSE FOR PREVENTION AND MITIGATION INVESTMENT

Our goal is to secure necessary funding to prevent or mitigate prioritized hazards. Safety and security improvement programming requires a chartered course. It is a journey that must address multiple risks and mitigation processes without disadvantage to the core mission of the community or the strategy of the organization. Projects will typically complement strategic direction. They ideally protect people, assets, critical processes, and brand reputation. The Security Executive Council's *Collective Knowledge: Business Continuity Program* notes "positive correlation between program drivers and program success" including:

- Regulatory
- Product
- Brand protection
- Incident
- Sponsor
- Geography
- Corporate culture
- ROI/value[3]

The direction for physical and logical access control programming is informed by multiple risk drivers. All must be taken into account and attended to. Incident reviews reveal security shortfalls and opportunity for protection reemphasis ranging from access control protocols to segregation of duties. Converged mitigation of access risk in both the physical and logical environments can meet future protection requirements against internal and external threats including the reach of organized crime. Unanticipated events require nimble investigative capability and need-to-know information sharing.

[3]Security Executive Council, "Collective Knowledge: Business Continuity Program."

Simultaneous emphasis on existing and evolving regulatory requirements and good practices made incremental security investments opportunistic. Interactive security and exception reporting appeared capable of redeeming all mitigation costs and contributing to the bottom line. Physical and logical access control, acceptable use, risk event, and code of conduct reporting enable ROI capability. Governance can help to assure sustainable good practices.

Overlapping risks and benefits may be required to obtain investment approval. Priority projects can feature multiple drivers. Holistic alignment may simultaneously support the organization mores and business plan. Mitigation solutions often require capital projects and expense investment. Chartering the project by identifying drivers with attendant costs and benefits is the first step in influencing investment.

Chartering enables goal setting with definition and purpose. "A goal establishes both a subjective and objective criterion for success ... first you define the goal and then it defines you."[4] Identifying champions for program and project charters should not be difficult. Prudent leadership sponsors understand their responsibility to protect people and assets, particularly when high-risk events occur. Even less enthusiastic patrons understand that compliance demands attention given the potential liability for inaction.

Remember the knowledge-based access diligence discussed in Chapter Three. In the next few pages, we will charter a related hypothetical headquarters (HQ) identity authentication and protection pilot that requires financing. We begin by diagramming the security solution for the proof-of-concept pilot and potential enterprise implementation. We aim to authenticate identity and vet reputation for those requiring access to a multinational headquarters (to the extent allowed by law, as international constraints vary). We have seen this objective in a number of existing and evolving global good security practices and compliance requirements. Figure 5.1 outlines a hypothetical HQ identity authentication and protection pilot.

Our purposes include the reduction of risk and existing mitigation costs, as well as introducing value added benefits such as identity insurance and identity theft reclamation services. The charter involves

---

[4]Westerby, *In Hostile Territory*.

Hypothetical HQ Identity Authentication and Protection Pilot

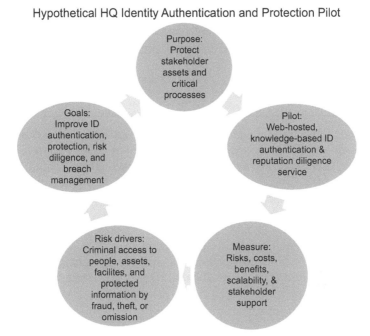

Figure 5.1 HQ Pilot. © Crime Prevention Associates. All rights reserved.

piloting the use of a knowledge-based, web-hosted service to replace current applicant and partner diligence processes. The solution will simultaneously enable breach management. Moreover, a successful pilot for internal use may be leveraged for additional testing as a revenue-producing customer offering. Measures will include risk, cost, benefit, stakeholder support, and return on investment.

The charter will generally mirror many of the elemental drivers of successful comprehensive business continuity planning. The proof-of-concept or pilot success will enable our hypothetical organization to keep insider threats to a minimum while arming stakeholders and customers with reasonable identity protection. It will also test an enterprise implementation for broader savings, cost avoidance, and incremental revenue.

5.2 COMMUNICATING THE BIG PICTURE

Identity theft risk is right behind personal injury and health hazard anxieties in our people-centric protection approach. Criminals who hack into networks or fraudulently gain access to protected stakeholder information put bank accounts, social insurance benefits, and reputations at risk. Indirect costs attributed to incident recovery, including victim time commitments and loss of productivity, compound direct losses.

William Morrow of Quarri Technologies summarized the dilemma and opportunity:

> Identity theft, fraud, and fabrication impact tens of millions of Americans resulting in business losses topping $56 billion a year. However, it is much more than money. Identity theft and data breaches impact people's lives and reputations. They impact a company's brand and consumer trust. These are assets you spend a lifetime building, that are easily damaged, and hard or impossible to repair. Responsible individuals and companies should have a comprehensive identity authentication and theft liability shield including state of the art background screening, customer identity validation, employee training, and breach mitigation and resolution plans. Identity theft is the fastest growing crime in the world.[5]

We cannot settle the risk of identity fraud and theft in property crime statistics alone. The integrity of the credential holder does not hazard just data and assets. On 9/11, we suffered the loss of too many lives to overlook the human consequences of a criminal act enabled by identity fraud. In the context of family, any avoidable injury or loss is enough to make the point. Numerous other examples of permissioned access within a community have resulted in mayhem.

Some are seemingly unrelated to your primary protection mission but have a way of introducing unanticipated risk. For instance, news of a campus shooter at Virginia Tech on April 16, 2007, caught worldwide attention. The Blacksburg, Virginia, event with 32 dead and dozens injured had global implications.[6] The diverse campus hosts students from 42 states in the United States and 35 other countries. Many communities had an immediate interest in ascertaining the safety implications for their members. Starbucks was no exception.

Early reports were sketchy. A number of partners were students and many others had sons, daughters, extended family, or friends on campus.

[5]William Morrow (executive chairman and CEO at Quarri Technologies, a security software company), in discussion with the author, 2009.
[6]Griffin, "Lessons from Virginia Tech."

Starbucks anticipated the need for management and security presence, supply chain requirements for memorial service support, and additional partners to operate the stores.

The rampage was conducted by Seung-Hui Cho, an English major, who had been judged mentally ill in 2005 after stalking female students. It ended with his suicide. He had easily acquired handguns and hundreds of rounds of ammunition. He left a ranting video that documented both his state of mind and homicidal intentions.

Virginia Tech and others reassessed their security. Virginia and US federal gun laws were influenced in the wake of the tragedy. Universities and corporations heard from stakeholders who were concerned about access control and managing the potential of an active shooter on campus. Many were moved to consider their entire security program, from screening to access control with exception reporting and response. All are subject to stakeholder expectations

5.3 CHARTER SUMMARY: THE ELEVATOR SPEECH

The following example in Figure 5.2 is a simplified charter summary for incremental security with return on investment. It is a hypothetical pilot. No capital is required. The hypothetical pilot proposes a web-based service to reauthenticate all headquarters personnel with permissioned access cards. The pilot would require 5,000 employees, contractors, and service providers to enroll via the network for interactive knowledge-based identity authentication.

In the hypothetical pilot in Figure 5.2, reputation integrity will be cross-referenced beyond traditional county criminal checks to national and multinational justice and corrections databases including fugitive warrants. Participant incentives include free identity protection and $25,000 per person identity theft insurance for one year. Total expense for the project is $27.50 per person or $137,500 including fully loaded labor costs for registration. Benefits are calculated at $190 per person. Savings and cost avoidance from the existing diligence practices, assuming successful results and a post-pilot enterprise implementation, would approach $4 million per year for an organization hiring 50,000 or more personnel. Cost avoidance is minimally estimated at $50 per person for labor productivity loss savings in the event of a security breach. Current international studies suggest identity recovery averages more than 200 hours.

Hypothetical Project Charter Summary	Description – Headquarters Pilot
Access Control	Identity Authentication and Protection Pilot
Purpose:	1. Employee and guest safety 2. Stakeholder and asset security 3. Policy and regulatory compliance 4. Diligence and breach cost reductions
Methodology: Cross-functional project team of Security, Human Resources, Legal Affairs, Finance, Communications, Procurement, and IT. Linked participation requirement for access control compliance featuring risk landscape tutorial, policy, regulatory requirements, and proactive identity protection benefit.	1. Proof: US Fair Credit Reporting Agency approved, secure, web-hosted, diligence for current access permissioned employees, service providers and contractors. 2. Authenticate their identities and register for free one-year identity protection and $25,000 in identity theft insurance.
Objectives: Protect people. Secure physical and virtual assets including information and critical dependent processes. Contribute margin. Enable business plan.	1. Improve employer of choice value proposition with safer, more secure environment. 2. Test post employment diligence to improve current screening incrementally at lower cost with scalable international capability to detect undisclosed conduct or fraud. 3. Test transition to proactive protection value proposition. 4. Assess implementation of pre-breach protection cost efficiency.

Return on Investment Calculation:
Required capital – None
Pilot Expenses: Subscription & Enrollment
for 5,000 personnel at $15 ea $75,000
Enrollment labor at ¼ hr $50 $62,500
Total Cost
$137,500
3-Year Cost Avoidance/Savings Benefits:
  1. Crime loss $
    100,000
  2. Voluntary turnover $
    50,000
  3. Claim litigation $
    100,000
  4. Breach management $
    200,000
  5. 2 hour productivity $
    500,000
  Total Benefit $
$950,000
	Assumptions:
	
	Significant residual risk remains with current access diligence for 4,000 proprietary personnel and 1,000 service personnel and contractors
	
	10% of historical loss
	10 voluntary resignations
	Defense cost mitigation
	Savings of $40 each credit protection
	2 hours productivity at $50 hour

Risk of Not Performing Pilot	1. Stakeholder and customer confidence 2. Injury, loss, and brand reputation

Figure 5.2 Charter Summary. © Crime Prevention Associates. All rights reserved.

A relevant charter narrative will accompany any summary to document historical risk costs and hypothetical residual risk based on issue history and benchmarked losses within industry or service organization segments. Executive sponsor interest may reside with the chief financial officer and the general counsel. Cross-functional project team members typically include representatives from communications, finance, human resources, legal, operations, and security. Quantitative cost and loss reduction measures will likely include regulatory and policy compliance. Qualitative benefits may be measured in stakeholder and consumer confidence, which affects brand loyalty and market performance.

The opportunity to deny crime with cost savings while enabling community productivity can be as compelling as incremental security proves cost-effective. The charter summary provides concise talking points for your elevator speech. Risk, cost, and benefit can be broadly covered in five floors. Rolf Sigg, the head of Siemens' billion dollar security business headquartered in Switzerland, good-humoredly reminded me that brevity was required for comparatively smaller building elevator rides in his country. Need-to-know information always must be reserved for more confidential spaces.

When the CEO, other chief-level executive, or peer asks you, "What's new?" your hook to the extended conversation may be, "We are exploring a means to incrementally improve access security while reducing risk and loss cost, with added potential for a new customer revenue stream." You may find a surprised listener who only anticipated being updated with the day's bad news. At any rate, you will not lose an influencing opportunity. Ideally, protection practitioners have regularly scheduled briefs with key executives. Summary communications help meetings that are subject to abbreviation. These are the briefs that begin with an executive apology such as, "I know we were scheduled for an hour, but I have an important engagement in 15 minutes."

Our cross-functional team approaches complement multiple-interest agendas. Finance is typically capable of offering persuasive project cost and benefit analysis. Legal support can lend credence to the risk liability discussion. Human resources has a vested interest in people protection and engagement enhancements, particularly if they are in a "pay for performance" environment, responsible for measurable engagement and turnover objectives. Communications can influence calendaring, messaging, and training. Operations will help determine the viability of change. All will have a stake in improved protection that features financial performance. Team members communicate objectives, gather input, and influence across the organization.

5.4 COSTS, LOSSES, AND BENEFITS DETERMINE RETURN ON INVESTMENT

Total cost of ownership for any solution should be anticipated prior to forecasting benefits. The hypothetical HQ pilot is a relatively exceptional, expense only request requiring no capital funding. Capital funds, particularly in depressed financial circumstances, are prized assets that must be competitively won with persuasive and compelling evidence of need. All expenses must be considered. It pays to align your programming with the chief financial officer or an influential lieutenant early on. CFOs are generally enthusiastic in their support for projects that can reduce risk and cost while improving operating margins. Transparency is key.

Expenses that are often overlooked include capital investment write-offs for replacement of assets still on the books, as well as training, maintenance, and monitoring. Total cost of ownership for a capital project will include project management, communications, training, maintenance, and depreciation. Your ability to capitalize depends on generally accepted accounting practices and policy. Exclusion of any pertinent consideration including life expectancy replacement costs can muddy the protection cost picture.

Wide calculation of benefits must also be undertaken. Recall the supply chain pilot in Chapter Three. Objective product risk analysis made the pragmatic case for prioritizing regulatory compliance within C-TPAT and ISO security guidelines. Incremental logistics security and quality assurance make sense for a critical supply chain. Disruption of supply including quality assurance is a potential show-stopper for any company. Authentication of talent and protection of identification are similarly strategic.

Transit of goods transparency eliminates theft or adulteration opportunities between the supplier, port facilities, and manufacturers. Authenticated goods and trusted personnel not only address concerns for weapons of mass destruction and illegal conversion of legitimate supply chains, they enable stakeholder and consumer quality assurance. Quantitative values forecasted first year return on investment anticipating that container integrity improvement would reduce inspections and their related costs. The concept closely follows Commissioner Bonner's idea for a "green lane," where extraordinary precautionary security measures would enable the private sector to speed processing by US Customs.[7]

5.5 MEASURE TWICE, CUT ONCE, AND REPORT

With the implementation of a pilot program, the carpenter's maxim most always applies: "Measure twice. Cut Once." Even small pilots may require objective, professional financial calculation as well as legal consultation. Aside from the penultimate risk considerations of human injury or death, enterprise implementation and potential liabilities may be millions of dollars. That is not to say that your back-of-a-paper-napkin intuitive calculations cannot be correct.

The person who signs a big check funding a project or strategic initiative likes to have the peace of mind that comes with rigorous analytical diligence. Proof of concept pilots to enterprise implementations require the total cost of ownership against all the potential benefits. Preexisting metrics for cost from average incidence, injury, damage, asset loss, business interruption, turnover, claims, etc. can be parlayed for benefit calculation with relatively simple mitigation assumptions.

Don't wait to be asked. Key stakeholder reporting ensures that the value of your cross-functional endeavor is understood over multiple reporting periods. Organizational leadership is apt to change. Institutional memory can be lost. Reminding invested stakeholders where you have been establishes credibility for future endeavors. George Campbell cautions us, "security metrics are not just about numbers; they are about performance … and will be measured with or without you."[8]

The lessons of the past continue to inform future security risk mitigation and should not be lost. The piloted proof-of-concept at Hardee's in the Philadelphia Roy Rogers market in 1993 did more than impact crime by 84 percent and propel a revenue increase of $34,000 per test unit. It also influenced capital investment in prevention and adoption of security practices for our wider enterprise as well as the quick service industry segment. After 1992, Hardee's robberies were reduced by 83 percent (Figure 5.3). This was due to the broad implementation of

[7]US Customs and Border Protection, "Securing the Global Supply Chain."
[8]Campbell, *Measures and Metrics in Corporate Security* (see chapt. 1, n. 11).

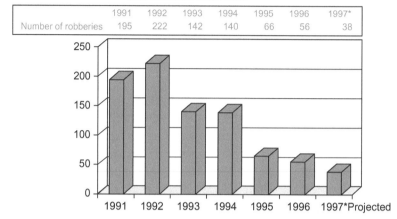

Hardee's Robbery Incidents

83% decrease since 1992

	1991	1992	1993	1994	1995	1996	1997*
Number of robberies	195	222	142	140	66	56	38

Figure 5.3 © Hardee's Food Systems, Inc. All rights reserved. Used with permission.

solutions such as security installations in all company-operated units; expanded crime and violence awareness training; and routine screening of applicants, employees being promoted, and probable-cause suspects pursuant to major losses.

Robbery violence was similarly diminished at 7-Eleven, Long John Silver's, Hardee's, and Starbucks Coffee.[9] Arguably hundreds if not thousands of physical and psychological injuries have been avoided in these businesses and their fast followers in convenience, quick service food, and small footprint retail. ROI was easily measured in millions of dollars in direct cost avoidance estimates including cash losses, inventory, and casualty claims.

Lagging indicators became leading indicators for commercial armed robbery risk. Robbery frequency closely followed average loss data. The Western Behavioral Sciences Institute originally pinned the amount of money available as a primary driver of robbery frequency at 7-Eleven. Dr. Rosemary Erickson of Athena Research reaffirmed those findings in the studies mentioned in Chapter 4.[10]

Table 5.1 clearly shows increased robber interest, 33 and 38 percent, for the adults and juveniles, respectively, for targets offering more than

[9]Wailgum, "Metrics for Corporate and Physical Security Programs."
[10]Erickson, *Teenage Robbers*, 6.

Table 5.1 The Least Dollar Amount for which Adult and Juvenile Robbers Would Attempt a Robbery

Dollar Amount	Adult Robbers		Juvenile Robbers	
	%Who Would Rob	Cumulative %	% Who Would Rob	Cumulative %
10	9	9	6	6
20	4	13	1	7
30	1	13	0	7
40	1	14	1	8
50	6	20	1	9
60	6	22	3	12
70	0	22	1	13
80	2	24	0	13
90	3	26	2	15
100	12	39	13	28
150	2	41	7	35
200	4	45	7	42
200 +	55	100	58	100

$200 cash. That bodes well for security service providers who produce products that feature cash control, time-delay, time-lock, and other smart-safe technology in a layered risk mitigation approach. Combined with courier service and in-store credit offered by banking partners, bill validated drops may relieve most risk exposure associated with cash, including trips to the bank. Indirect benefits may be calculated from labor savings for cash counts, banking, and shortage investigations, as well as turnover reductions associated with high risk cash handling. The reader should note that some robbers will not be deterred or dissuaded, thus making violence avoidance training a similarly reasonable investment.

We first correlated the turnover reduction benefit at Southland in 1980. Analysis of the six most improved store divisions for robbery showed a 25 percent average incident reduction and a corresponding 12 percent decrease in personnel turnover. In contrast, the six least improved divisions experienced a 28 percent increase in robbery and an 18 percent increase in turnover. The security program impact was in the millions of dollars even before calculating injury, cash, and liability cost improvements.[11]

[11]D'Addario, *Loss Prevention through Crime Analysis*, 74.

Do not rest on your laurels. Success does not diminish opportunities to influence program adoption. Diverse global organizations sometimes get distracted with cultural, geographical, and ideological differences rather than staying in tune with common denominator objectives. Sometimes the risk agenda gets reprioritized. Market maturity, relative experience, and economic circumstances qualify support or lack thereof for individual mitigation programs within the security portfolio. Local risk perception and solution confidence are all important. Timing is also an issue. Crime incidence generally rises in an extended economic downturn and conversely diminishes with prosperity. More focused interest in security options may correspond with increased injury, asset loss, and profit contraction. When the core mission of the community is distracted or constrained by crime, effective security practices can re-enable.

5.6 EXCEPTION DETECTION ENABLES THE CORE BUSINESS

Paradigms are rapidly changing. Alarm monitoring by central stations no longer ensures police response in most major cities. False alarms and strapped public safety resources combine to fuel innovation and innovative transition from a model that no longer works. Protection designers and risk managers are likely to change service level expectations and agreements in light of this phenomenon. No one is likely to be caught in the act but virtual accountability is more certain.

Coincidentally, ROI-capable exception reporting and accountability are on the rise. Retailers have authenticated point-of-sale investigation values between $1414 and $7500 per case with up to 91 percent accountability for detectable embezzlers and fraudsters. Integrated smart technologies including cash controllers and digital video recorders assure consequences.

Stores, banks, and critical facilities of the future will likely feature some mix of digital video, audio, and transaction analytics to authenticate personnel, customers, and service providers with access control peripherals. Alarm monitoring facilities will arguably transition to exception detection and reporting facilities capable of determining access, casualty claim, crime, delivery, inventory, and other transaction anomalies including utility usage.

8.Discreet duress communications

Store of the Future
Risk-Based Mitigation
Considerations

1.Manmade and natural risk assessment

7. DVR NVR video/audio analytics

2. CPTED/Risk mitigation design

6. Point-of-sale exception reporting

3. Access control & identity diligence

9. Risk detection, reporting, & mitigation communications center for safety, security, & quality.

10. Other

5. Inventory control

4. Cash control or courier services

Figure 5.4 Store of the Future. © Crime Prevention Associates. All rights reserved.

People, asset, and critical process protection will feature risk-based design with exception documentation that will preserve events and data with economical resource conservation. Network requirements will be amended from piping live video or audio to more economical message packets that will be reviewed for cost mitigation opportunities including referral of criminal cases and reward offers. See Figure 5.4.

Considerations for the store of the future will play for both bricks and mortar and virtual venues. People and transaction authentication will assure accountability for loss control and revenue protection.

5.7 ESTIMATING NET RETURN ON INVESTMENT

Consider adopting a loss cost plus protection cost strategy to enable scaled reporting based on traditional organization metrics such as cost or benefit per person, per unit, or per operating square footage. Rolled-up total cost or benefit as a percentage of sales or profit may

Hypothetical Cost and Benefit Measures for ROI

Period Metric	Value	Description
Facility count Square footage Personnel count	1,406 2,833,500 31,176	Wholly owned operations: 1,389 stores, 1 headquarters, 5 regional offices, 9 manufacturing and distribution facilities
Gross sales Net revenue	$1.4B $42M	Global gross sales Global net revenue
Gross security contribution	$14.36M	Security system ROI $7.03M Cost avoidance, $6.71M case development & claims asset recovery $.62M
Security staff expense + 3rd party services Total security cost	$1.6M $2.1M $3.7M	16 personnel, benefits, travel, education, depreciation, etc. Security monitoring ($.60M), officers ($1.2M), courier services ($.31M), etc.
100% cash 50% inventory Total profit and loss cost	$1.4M $1.7M $3.1M	Cash loss due to embezzlement, theft, robbery, & burglary 50% of all inventory shrink, due to theft, assumes 50% mis-ship, damage, and inventory error
Estimated net security contribution	$7.56M	Gross security contribution ($14.36M) minus total security cost ($3.7M) and minus total profit and loss cost ($3.1M0) = ($7.56M)
Estimated net return on investment	$2.04	Net contribution $7.56M/total security cost ($3.7M) = $2.04 return per dollar invested

Figure 5.5 ROI Chart. © Crime Prevention Associates. All rights reserved.

assist year-to-year reporting and benchmarking between organizations. The cost and benefit of security become certain within the organizational context. More importantly the contribution of security to the operating mission, strategy, and business plan becomes clear. See Figure 5.5.

Our hypothetical security ROI case above offers $2.04 return on every dollar invested. It is well within the capability of retail-based security units that have documented returns exceeding two to one. Estimates for my teams have run as high as $2.63 for annual contribution per dollar invested. Retail operators have the advantage of well-documented cost and loss metrics within their operating profit and loss statements.

Estimated Net Contribution = Estimated Gross Contribution
− (Total Security Cost + P&L Loss Cost)
Estimated Net Return on Investment
− Net Contribution/Total Security Cost

Annual core metrics allow easy calculations of total security or benefit per gross revenue or profit dollar, person, facility, or operating square footage for multiple periods.

ROI assumptions will ideally be tested against the performance of objectively selected control groups and retested over time for revalidation. Please note that tangible cost only is included in our hypothetical model. No allowance is made for intangible security contributions that may include crisis prevention, injury and turnover cost reductions, compliance fines, or related litigation cost avoidance. Mitigated frequency and severity of criminal events in any community can drive ROI calculation. Under no circumstances does periodic success guarantee future results. Risk prevention and mitigation are an ongoing opportunity.

Our security viability will always be tested. Threats to people and assets will continue to evolve to defeat designed mitigation. Common criminals, self-proclaimed freedom fighters, and terrorists will resort to extortion, kidnapping, narcotics trafficking, robbery, and theft to fund their criminal enterprises. Accidents and natural disasters will always happen. Development of measured risk mitigation and effective infrastructure investment can level the playing field. Imagine if product and service costs reflected a 50 percent reduction in fraud and loss cost. The resultant multibillion-dollar windfall could seed needed preparedness infrastructure improvement.

Surveying available industry data and segment peers for risk assessments, mitigation solutions, and evaluation methodology is helpful. Established benchmarks for percentage of gross revenue dedicated to security within your business segment can justify spending. Competitors with superior security may likely impair your ability to perform by deflecting criminal activity to your place of business. Those who are better prepared to mitigate all hazards will recover sooner, serve their stakeholders better, and earn brand reputation.

Discussion Exercise

Identify the elements of a security project or program recently implemented or under consideration in your community, including:

Project goal(s)
Issue history
Cost: capital and expense
Quantitative and qualitative benefits
Risk of not funding
Pilot or proof of concept description

Leadership champion(s)
Project manager
Cross-functional team members
Communications plan and implementation schedule
Additional Information and Resources
1. US Federal Trade Commission, Consumer Information: Identity Theft: http://www.consumer.ftc.gov/features/feature-0014-identity-theft.
2. CSID, Identity Protection: Overview: http://www.csid.com/identity-protection/.
3. George K. Campbell, *Measures and Metrics in Corporate Security* (Security Executive Council, 2006): https://www.securityexecutivecouncil. com/secstore/index.php?main_page = product_info&products_id = 324.
4. Rosemary Erickson, *Teenage Robbers: How and Why They Rob* (Athena Research, 2003): http://athenaresearch.com/materials/prchs_trhwr.pdf.

●●●
_____

"US v. LAM PHAM – Thang Van Nguyen ... was sentenced ... to 78 months in prison, five years of supervised release and $1,000,000 in restitution for Bank Fraud. PHAM was the leader of a ring operating in Southern California that committed more than $1.6 million in bank fraud using the stolen identities and bank account numbers of 102 different individuals, most of whom were Starbucks employees. A Starbucks Human Resources Employee, M.T. ... was sentenced to 42 months in prison and 5 years of supervised release. M.T. accessed a computer system to steal the employee info used in the account takeovers."[12]

All funds lost by victims were restored by the banks.

Compensatory identity and credit protection was offered to all affected by the breach. The case influenced improved controls and additional protection investment. It also informed understanding of loss cost including the time and resources required to repair identity theft. By the end of 2007, total P&AP contribution was calculated at more than two to one on investment. Contribution analysis remains a work in progress.

ROI remains calculable for both the physical and logical environments. Some will be persuaded by their own ethical compass to do the right thing with a comprehensive approach to good practices. Others will be nudged to mitigate risk just in time by vicarious learning, compliance requirements, or even liability.

_____

[12]The US Attorney's Office, "Prosecution Priorities for ID Theft Working Group."

CHAPTER 6

Leveraging Data to Lead with Good Practices

Learning from our own lessons and those of others requires discipline. It's more than just numbers. Surveys, benchmarks, and case studies can inform us of multiple dimensions. They may shed light on risk frequency or severity, mitigation effectiveness, how we perform against objectives and against our peers, and good and best practices. They enable our clientele to provide valuable feedback. When properly connected to the mission of the organization, they can influence collaboration for results.

"'Vicarious learning' is the notion that people can and will learn through being given access to the learning experiences of others."[1] A collaborative project by researchers at four British universities, Edinburgh, Newcastle, Sheffield, and Sussex, aimed to learn more about how and why vicarious learning works. Through a web-based multimedia database known as PATSy, researchers made a virtual patient available to trainees, educators, clinicians, and researchers.

If only security and safety protection practitioners had the instruments to persuasively forecast looming or residual risk. Like legendary clinicians, we could diagnose the patient and mitigate the life-threatening condition just in time for a happy ending. Unfortunately, there is no single solution for an all-hazards risk, detection, and mitigation diagnostic.

Voluminous published data resides within our reach, informing us of the consequences of protection failure. For example, food contamination in recent years has taken a toll on confidence. Tainted baby formula, fruit, lettuce, peanut products, spinach, and other foods, raw and prepared, have sickened or killed thousands of humans, animals, and household pets. The culprits include E. coli, melamine, salmonella, and other hazards that we have added to our risk awareness vocabulary.

Mitigation for food-borne illness is not out of our reach. It merely requires testing for known toxins throughout the food chain. ConAgra, the maker of Peter Pan and Great Value peanut butter, estimated the

---

[1]Teaching and Learning Research Programme, "Vicarious Learning."

cost of their 2007 voluntary product recall at \$50 to \$60 million.[2] Green job incentives ought to include regulatory personnel who will ensure that damaged products are destroyed on premises or only reshipped for approved alternate use (animal feed) or destruction. Not surprisingly, consumer confidence in food safety dropped.[3]

Historical data has implications for security practitioners from the economic front. According to the monthly Consumer Confidence Survey conducted by the Conference Board, consumer confidence in the United States hit an all-time low in February 2009.[4] Escalating unemployment, personal financial crises, layoffs, and downsizing led to increased crime and violence and constrained regulatory activity that would otherwise enable early detection, mitigation, or account-ability. (Since that dramatic drop in 2009, consumer confidence rebounded in June 2013 to its highest level since January 2008.[5])

6.1 SURVEYS AND BENCHMARKS

Surveys can be very effective for mitigating risk. They enable you to comprehend attitudes, data, and circumstances that require attention and understanding. Survey data may range from risk awareness to post-crisis security confidence. It may include actionable information for risk mitigation.

Investigative questionnaires are one means for polling prospective witnesses and suspects following a reported incident. They allow engagement of broad or remote communities on a timely basis to demonstrate that a risk event has been detected and accountability or mitigation processes are underway. They can also provide anonymous reporting options or incentivize information sharing with rewards. Most importantly, investigative surveys engage community members to reinforce the notion that their protection is important while enabling them to participate in potential solutions.

My teams have effectively combined questionnaire and reward incentive offers to solve burglary, controlled substance, embezzlement,

---

[2]Reynolds, "ConAgra Estimates Peanut Butter Recall."
[3]Shine, "Consumer Confidence in Food Safety Drops."
[4]Rooney, "Consumer Confidence Plummets."
[5]Isidore, "Consumer Confidence at 5-Year High."

homicide, robbery, product tampering, threats, and other high-risk inquiries by polling potential witnesses for unknown details. A simple declarative statement describing the event is followed by a request to detail (who, what, when, where, how, and why) knowledge about the event.

For instance:

> On August 20, 2013, unauthorized product labeled as "Satan's Elixir" was discovered at shipping station #44 between 01:30 and 04:00 hours. Please detail what you know about this incident (who, what, when, where, how, and why) in the space provided below. Seal the envelope and return it to your supervisor. Information leading to actionable accountability may also be reported anonymously to 1-800-QUALITY and be eligible for a reward up to $1,000.00.

Questionnaires and surveys inform. They can nimbly communicate risk or mitigation and simultaneously remind clients of core values, standards, reporting channels, and resources to maintain accountability and enable mission. Your ability to these things in concert enables early risk detection and mitigation that will ultimately define brand reputation.

Other formats shape or collect value perceptions of products or services rendered or identify improvement opportunities. Still others help determine relative performance in a peer group or market niche. If you want to know where you are and where you need to be, you have to ask. Surveys and benchmarks serve this purpose when comparative data is relevant. A benchmark can be defined as "a standard or point of reference against which things may be compared or assessed."[6]

Client survey input is always valuable for discerning attitudes for both the risk environment and security practices. Surveying groups operated around the clock in a full range of relative risk conditions including exposure to crime can provide valuable insights. Business operators typically execute daily security protocols to protect themselves and their customers. Their responsibilities routinely include access control, audits, as well as risk event and suspicion reporting, first responder and community agency relations, and security technology troubleshooting.

---

[6]*Oxford Pocket Dictionary of Current English*, 2nd ed., s.v. "benchmark."

One retail security attitude survey conducted in 2007 at Starbucks yielded an impressive 89 percent response from targeted managers. The survey target audience informed the survey team of their overwhelming agreement that the company cared about keeping its employees and customers safe from crime (above 90 percent). Moreover, the operators felt safe in their stores and would refer a family member or friend knowing they would be safe. Most agreed that their current employment was safer than their previous experience. No doubt, attitudes for safety and security benefit the cultural phenomenon of care. The results will serve as a benchmark for future performance.

At Starbucks, enterprise engagement was high in 2007. The company was ranked 16th on *Fortune* magazine's 100 Best Companies to Work For.[7] The P&AP group also registered world class engagement. The data from Maslow to Gallup is persuasive. Cared-for, self-actualized individuals build strong communities.

Engagement is closely related to job satisfaction. Both metrics can be associated with quality assurance and the general success of a business enterprise. Costs and losses can be contained when personnel don't churn. The employer's nemesis, job dissatisfaction, can be predictive of employee turnover and negative behaviors ranging from poor customer service to product quality alteration and theft.

John Clark and Richard Hollinger provided landmark data in 1983 that has not been refuted. "Unhappiness with one's supervisors is the most important dimension of the eight different factors of job dissatisfaction that we examined in predicting both employee dishonesty and counterproductive behavior. Specifically, retail employees who steal either property or time from the firm are more likely to believe that a supervisor is ... unsuccessful at getting people to work together; unfriendly; unhelpful at getting [the employee's] job done; incompetent at his or her own job; and unconcerned about the welfare of those working under them."[8]

---

[7]*Fortune Magazine*, "100 Best Companies to Work For 2007."
[8]Clark Hollinger, *Theft by Employees in Work Organizations*.

6.2 CASE STUDY: USING BENCHMARKS TO SUPPORT A SECURITY PROPOSAL

When benchmarking outside your organization, professional associations are one source for good and best security practices. ASIS International (ASIS), the Association for Certified Fraud Examiners (ACFE), the International Security Managers Association (ISMA), the National Retail Federation (NRF), the Retail Industry Leaders Association (RILA), and the Security Executive Council (SEC) are just a few of the groups that provide knowledge exchanges and benchmarking opportunities. Public demographic data, including crime, is also available for comparative analysis.

In addition to peer benchmarking, companies can participate annually in a number of broader industry niche surveys. Retailers may opt for NRF's annual National Retail Security Survey (NRSS).[9] The NRSS reported $41.6 billion in retail losses for 2006. The results, compiled by Hollinger's University of Florida team, shared loss and security cost data from 139 retail enterprises, without attribution. The data comprises a health check for retail operators and reports both loss and security cost trends.

Using the 2006 NRSS and other benchmarks, the following case study (Figures 6.1–6.7) represents select data for a $3.5 billion, small-footprint retail organization. In this case, the new Loss Prevention (LP) team developed risk and mitigation considerations for dynamic crime conditions that threaten the potential prosperity of the enterprise. The LP team intends to influence management with a combination of internal reporting metrics compared with industry, peer, and government data. Their objective is to make the persuasive case for resource reallocation to fund an ROI-capable security strategy.

Though the data in this example case study is from 2006–2008, its structure and format can be modeled using more current research on topics that fit your organization's specific needs.

The exercise demonstrates a proposal to address compelling robbery, burglary, and theft risks with professional LP staff and capital improvements using funds currently earmarked for security officers. Peer and industry benchmarks including the NRSS results support the

---

[9]Grannis, "Retail Losses Hit $41.6 Billion."

Case Study: Requestor Executive Summary

Current State: Robberies, Burglaries, and Internal Theft
- Robberies up 92% Year over Year (YOY), '06 to '07, up 400% Year to Date (YTD) in '08 Vs. '07
- Burglaries up 156% YOY, '06 to '07, losses increased from $1.6M in '06 to $5.1M in '07, up 156%
- Losses due to internal theft average $5K+ per incident, More than 3X the national retail average

Current Spend: Operating and Capital Security Expense
- Requestor spends 80% less on Loss Prevention payroll than the industry average
- Requestor spends 400% more than the industry on contract services, specifically, security officers. In '07, Requestor spent almost $8M on officers, about 44% of the security contract services budget. FY08 budget was $12M, currently trending to exceed $17M.
- Existing Capital budget of $4.2M is insufficient to ensure safety and security of all at risk locations.

Retail Loss Prevention (LP) ASK
- 16 additional Full Time Equivalents (FTEs) in '08, $2.2M in payroll.
- $8.2M increase in capital funding.

Retail Spend Benefits
- Safety and Security benefit for retail employees ensuring Best Place to Work.
- $13.2M total combined annual savings and cost avoidance
    - $3.7M annual savings from increased identification and recovery from internal investigations.
    - $9M reduction against current trend in contract security expenditures.
    - $500K annual savings from burglary incidents.

Figure 6.1 Requestor Executive Summary. © Crime Prevention Associates. All rights reserved.

Requestor Robbery Frequency Comparison

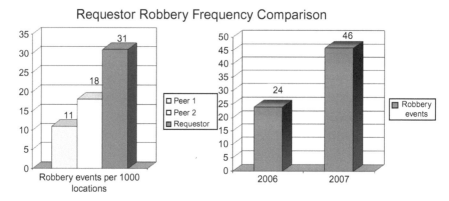

- Requestor suffered a 92% increase in robbery events between 2006 and 2007
- Requestor experiences almost 3 times the number of robbery events as Peer 1
- As robbery event frequency escalates so does the risk for increased violence
- It is critical to respond to correct our issue now that it has been clearly identified

Figure 6.2 Requestor Robbery Frequency Comparison. © Crime Prevention Associates. All rights reserved.

mitigation strategy for return on investment. The company in question is identified as "Requestor."

Figure 6.1 shows an executive summary with a call to action for changes in the security strategy. Robbery, burglary, and theft data is

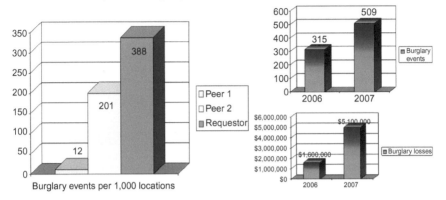

Requestor Burglary Frequency/Cost Comparison

>Burglary events are becoming more frequent and profitable for the perpetrator
>Product losses from burglary events in 2007 exceeded $3.2.M, a 156% increase over 2006
>Damage repair costs from burglary events exceeded $420K in 2006 and $1.8M in 2007 (above figures include burglary repair costs)
>Requestor experiences 50% more burglary events than our nearest competitor
>Effective burglary prevention involves adding time to the process for the potential offender

Figure 6.3 Requestor Burglary Frequency. © Crime Prevention Associates. All rights reserved.

Requestor and Prevention Industry Comparison: Staffing

	NRRSS Average	Requestor
Retail sales	$3.5B	$3.5B
Payroll expense as a % to sales (LP personnel)	.24	.05
LP Payroll $	$8.4M	$1.7M

>NRSS respondents average spend on loss prevention staffing is .24% of company sales
>Requestor currently spends .05% of company sales on loss prevention staffing
>Requestor spends 80% less than the national average on loss prevention staffing

Figure 6.4 Comparison. Staffing. © Crime Prevention Associates. All rights reserved.

effectively compared with peer organizations to demonstrate dispro-portionate risks including the frequency and cost of crime. Benchmark NRSS staffing and security service data support potential cost avoid-ance and loss prevention opportunities.

Requestor Investigative Capacity with Industry Comparison

Case Value
Current loss admissions are exceeding the initial evidentiary value by 250%
For every $1.00 we have when we begin an investigation, we develop $2.50

LP Manager Case Capacity
Each LP manager position is capable of resolving over $415K in losses annually
At current staffing levels requestor will be unable to investigate 1,350 potential internal losses
At current staffing levels requestor risks $7M in potential investigations remaining unresolved

NRSS Average		Requestor		Unresolved Investigation Risk	
Investigations per $100M in sales	50	Investigators	5	Requestor sales revenue	$3.5B
Requestor sales revenue	$3.5B	Annual investigation capability	80	Investigations per $100M in sales	50
Expected investigations w/ requestor sales volume	1,750	Total current investigation capability	400	Expected investigations w/ requestor sales volume	1,750
Expected investigations value w/ NRSS average @ $1,238 per investigation	$2.2M	Expected investigation value w/ requestor @ $5,182 per investigation	$2.1M	Probable investigation value requestor actual @ $5,182 per investigation	$9.1M
				Unresolved loss	$7M

Figure 6.5 Comparison: Investigative Capacity. © Crime Prevention Associates. All rights reserved.

Requestor Industry Comparison: Noncapital Expense (Contract Services)

NRSS Average		Requestor 2007 Actual		Difference	
Sales Revenue	$3.5B	Sales Revenue	$3.5B	Sales Revenue	$3.5B
Noncapital Expense (Contract Services)	.11	Noncapital Expense (Contract Services)	.51	Noncapital Expense (Contract Services)	.40
Noncapital Expense (Contract Services)	$3.9M	Noncapital Expense (Contract Services)	$17.9M	Noncapital Expense (Contract Services)	$14M

> Requestor currently disproportionately outspends the industry
> Requestor currently spends 44% of the contract services expense on Armed and Unarmed security officers
> Requestor Loss Prevention seeks to reduce spending on officers by a minimum of 10% in 2008 to allow full staffing of LP Managers

Figure 6.6 Comparison: Noncapital Expense. © Crime Prevention Associates. All rights reserved.

Requestor Physical Security Capital Needs

Initiative by Priority	Status	Target Locations	Deploy Cost	Implement Time	Metrics
1) Lock Boxes	Planning Sample received Vendor identified	1,469 Standing All Go Forward	$675K	90-120 Days	Reduces accessible cash in the event of a robbery. Allows for local drops of large denomination bills. <u>Average incident loss value</u>
2) Public View Monitors	Pilot (32 locations) 1/25/08 1st Install	500 Standing All Go Forward	$875K	3-6 Months	Provide a visual awareness and deterrent to all individuals entering the location. <u>Incident frequency reduction</u>
3) Signage -CCTV -Cash -Identification	Planning Sample received	1,469 Standing All Go Forward	$74K	30-45 Days	Provides a visual deterrent to potential perpetrators. <u>Incident frequency reduction</u>
4) Cash Counting Devices	Pilot (15 locations) 12/10/07 1st Install	1,469 Standing All Go Forward	$441K	90-120 Days	Reduces exposure due to counting large sums of cash. <u>Average incident loss value, Payroll hours</u>
5) DVR Upgrade	Locations Identified	193 Standing All Go Forward	$733K	90-120 Days	Reduces identification and closure time for identified issues. <u>Investigation closure time</u>
		Total Deployment Cost	$2.7M		

Figure 6.7 Capital Needs. © Crime Prevention Associates. All rights reserved.

The requestor seeks to mitigate significant robbery, burglary, and theft trends that are extraordinarily higher than year-over-year incidence reported by the FBI. Preliminary data for crime in the United States indicated that comparable crime category data actually decreased between 2006 and 2007.[10] The Requestor proposal seeks to win approval for $2.2 million in staffing and $8.2 million in security equipment capital investment. The proposal positions the requestor for $13.2 million in annual savings and cost avoidance.

Executive summaries must be supported by details. Risk comparisons, loss frequency, cost, and mitigation capability should be demonstrated. Peer company data is persuasive for illustrating these when available. As you can see in Figure 6.2, peer company robbery frequency per thousand locations is much less than Requestor experience.

Also, Requestor robbery incidents increased extraordinarily, by 92 percent, between 2006 and 2007. In comparison, the FBI annual crime data demonstrated a 1.2 percent decrease in robbery nationwide for

---

[10]Federal Bureau of Investigation, "Crime Statistics 2007."

the comparable period. The Requestor's data illustrates significant violence, losses, and risk to brand reputation.

Figure 6.3 shows us that Requestor burglary frequency is significantly higher than its peers. Once again, Requestor's year-over-year frequency trend is not driven by a national crime trend. The FBI crime data indicates burglary is down 0.8 percent for the period. Perhaps most importantly, product losses and damage costs appear to increase even faster. Together they imply a significant concern for getting product to market when inventory is unavailable to sell or crime-damaged facilities are taken off line for repair.

Requestor experience, combined with peer data and national crime trends, illustrate the priority risks that require mitigation. Industry segment data sheds light on benchmark security practices. Requestor proprietary metrics along with the NRF's NRSS findings provide insight for standard mitigation practices including staffing and security service levels.

The NRSS survey data establishes the average loss prevention staff payroll expense, which is well above Requestor's current investment. See Figure 6.4.

Survey data exposes a gap that supports Requestor staff expansion. This finding is developed to address both risk mitigation capacity and the ROI strategy.

Additional sales and profit risk may be mitigated by loss prevention staff. See Figure 6.5.

Requestor's disproportionate staffing constrains investigative and asset recovery capabilities. Even though Requestor is comparatively understaffed, investigative results are higher than the NRSS average. Arguably, expanded capacity also improves deterrence as accountability is improved.

Figure 6.6 illustrates that Requestor security service expenses are well above the NRSS data.

The disposition of security service expense is significant by virtue of its apparent inability to check the crime issues that are threatening personnel and the financial viability of the retail enterprise. This is a key influence opportunity. Requestor strategy requires these funds to underwrite staff and best practice security capital equipment.

Physical security capital needs are detailed to "target harden" store facilities. Cash drop lock boxes and cash-counting technology are intended to reduce the amount of money available. The proposal also includes public flat screen digital monitors, digital video recorders, and signage, which convey surveillance and event recording capability. All are associated with potential metrics to prove this prevention and mitigation strategy. See Figure 6.7.

Successfully preventing or impeding robbery, burglary, and theft is no small undertaking. The $13.2 million in savings and cost avoidance proposition introduced in Figure 6.1 may contribute to other quantitative and qualitative value. The data could be further supported with likely indirect benefits such as injury, counseling, and turnover cost reductions that closely follow reduction of crime incidence. Workers compensation and third party liability claims are two P&L lines that will typically be managed by others but will be credited to security when payouts recede. As we saw in the cost and benefit measures at Starbucks in Chapter Five, trained investigative staff can add millions of dollars in cost avoidance by providing evidence to deny specious claims. Digital video capability makes stakeholders feel cared for and criminals more likely to be held accountable.

As you can see, Requestor has boldly communicated both risk and remedy with aspirations of benchmark performance. Success is not automatic. Settling on the desired outcomes is only one step to influencing organizational behavior. In the end "good practices" security enables associates, customers, and the business to survive and thrive. Inventory is available to sell. Sales floors are not taken off line because they are crime scenes. Personnel feel less victimized and likely more engaged. Employees who are treated well treat customers in a similar fashion. If Clark and Hollinger are right, they are less likely to steal because their employer, particularly their manager, cares about them.

6.3 LEADERSHIP COURAGE AND COLLABORATION

Benchmarking isn't just about the numbers. Situational risk and mitigation must be carefully considered. The Requestor benchmarking case study clearly cast doubt on the efficacy of security officers deterring or preventing robbery and burglary for this small retail footprint.

Security officers are capable of impacting risk and enabling mitigation in appropriate circumstances. Coordinated deployment can improve results. For instance, well trained, properly equipped security officers can be integrated with a more comprehensive program to complement proprietary loss prevention and public safety resources. Such services can effectively augment security for alarm response that is not provided by public law enforcement. Temporary assignment of officers may also be prudent and valuable in the wake of a violent crime or natural disaster until longer-term countermeasures are implemented.

Before identifying a potential solution we have to prudently determine that we have a problem, or perhaps more hopefully, an opportunity. "We" is the operant word. Leadership courage is required when influencing management. Security officer deployment is often an emotional reaction by a well-intentioned operations executive in lieu of other solutions. Protection professionals must use relevant data persuasively to make the case for the holistic integrated approach to advance the organizational mission with economy and results.

The business, law enforcement, and community are stakeholders. Ensuring that all are on the same page accomplishes two objectives. First and foremost, it demonstrates responsibility. Second, it recognizes that true crime prevention, like any risk mitigation, is a collaborative affair. This was the approach taken at Southland in the late-1970s and 1980s. In those days, convenience stores were dubbed "stop and robs." Zoning officials delayed or denied building permits citing risk to public safety.

Ray Johnson, former "bad guy" and original data provider for the 1975 WBSI robbery deterrence study,[11] was presented to the media by Southland Public Affairs. His story was compelling. Ray had written a book titled *Too Dangerous to Be at Large* that detailed his criminal career up to and including his escape from Folsom Prison. Ray's delivery of the crime prevention approach for creating visibility, controlling cash, impeding escape routes, along with the dos and don'ts of violence avoidance was entertaining and effective. He became a frequent guest of Johnny Carson's on *The Tonight Show*. The results were amazing. Police departments and community zoning boards began to recognize the 7-Eleven approach more as a public safety solution than a problem. Customers connected that the cleaner, brighter, uncluttered look

---

[11]Crow and Bull, *Robbery Deterrence* (see chap. 4, n. 7).

of CPTED was connected to their safety. The customer tolerance for time-delay vending machines grew as robbers visited less frequently.

The Southland team developed and introduced a robbery prevention kit that included armed robber description forms, exit door frame height indicators, and cash protocol including the use of bait bills in cash drawers and deposits. Violence prevention tips were posted in the bathroom to remind everyone that their personal safety was a priority. Lower merchandise gondolas, signage control, lighting improvement, and safes up front incorporated the best elements of CPTED for natural surveillance. Premises featured a clean, bright, and vigilant look that translated to put criminals on stage for a precipitous reduction of robberies and robbery homicides as national crime rates were climbing. Criminal suspect description training enabled more arrests and convictions. The US Small Business Administration (SBA) virtually adopted the Southland robbery and violence prevention program. It fundamentally influenced the benchmark for late-night retail security.[12]

Similar community-facing practices have been introduced by other retailers, including Target. Brad Brekke, vice president of Assets Protection, coordinates strategic efforts to enhance safe and healthy communities for the Minnesota-based retailer. Safe City, modeled after a successful UK program, coordinates retail, security, and public safety resources for effective community protection. Activities range from community risk and mitigation education awareness to assisting local law enforcement with forensic and other technical resources.[13] In 2005, Target was presented with with the FBI's Minneapolis Division Director's Community Leadership Award.[14]

Mike Howard, general manager for global security, and his talented team at Microsoft take internal and external collaboration to the multinational enterprise level. They share best practices for their global security operations centers with all sectors. Under their mantra, "Protection. Technology. Value," Howard's group leverages Microsoft products and key technology partnerships to mitigate worldwide personnel and facility risks for value-added brand protection. Howard's risk mitigation brain trust gathered for a *Security Technology Executive* cover article in April

---

[12]Occupational Safety and Health Administration (OSHA), *Recommendations for Workplace Violence Prevention Programs*.
[13]Bridges, "Retailer Target Branches Out."
[14]Federal Bureau of Investigation (FBI), "Minneapolis Division Director's Award Recipients."

2009 (see Figure 6.8).[15] That September they shared their approach at the annual ASIS conference in Anaheim, California.

6.4 IDENTIFYING GOOD PRACTICES

Those of us who mitigate risk are happy to say we are in the continuous improvement business. Assembling an all-hazards mitigation program is an audacious undertaking that does not begin with Six Sigma. It starts with the notion of incremental improvement. Best practices may be an aspiration, but good and proven practices accomplish our goals. The British are fond of "good practice" nomenclature. The understatement still brings the implied warranty of results.

In a book I wrote in the late 1990s, *The Manager's Violence Survival Guide*, I took a basics approach to good practices to inform small business managers of the risk of workplace violence.[16] The mitigation elements of CPTED, violence avoidance, incident reporting, crime scene protection, household safety, and security were collected as a small business resource. There is not a lot that hasn't been done before. The trick is documenting the practice and result.

International standards increasingly rely on documentation. Risk mitigations for information technology, finance, operations, and supply chain continue to evolve with auditable process and results confirmation. Risk, incidence, loss, and benefit data are necessary to guide and measure mitigation practices for large and small communities.

We will see in Chapter Seven that governance enables compliance. Reorganizations, acquisitions, and leadership turnover will continue to churn the players, but mission, vision, values, policy, and compliance will continue to tell the tale for sustainable institutions. Things that we ought to do will be legislated for compliance—particularly after egregious losses involving critical infrastructure players.

Holistic mitigation requires anticipating any weak link. Our adversaries do. Criminals exploit network and program weakness like running water finds the crack in a dam. Good practice must be extended from one end of the spectrum to the other, from origin-country supply procurement, through manufacturing and distribution, to the customer

[15]Blades, "No Size Fits All."
[16]D'Addario, *Manager's Violence Survival Guide.*

Figure 6.8 STE Cover Image. © *Security Technology Executive.* All rights reserved.

service transaction and banking. If your supply chain is dependent on a trucking company to transport raw materials required for high-quality consumer products, you had better know that firm is ISO, C-TPAT, or Food Defense compliant.[17] Caring organizations inspect what they expect. Security requirements will be similar for proprietary and third-party entities regardless of size.

6.5 A CONVERGED APPROACH

Risk mitigation approaches in the physical and logical environments should be complementary in order to reach a desired state of security. Barb Padagas, manager of information, privacy, and IT security, expects her Puget Sound Energy network environment to be as robust as the physical premises security when her stakeholders are conversant with risk, vulnerabilities, and compliance requirements. Customers, service providers, and other authorized personnel can rely on need-to-know data availability, confidentiality, and integrity when safeguards are in place. Stakeholders understand that energy production is less likely to be compromised or interrupted when the right combination of administrative, physical, and technical controls are perfected within national compliance requirements and internationally recognized security standards.

According to the ISO 27000 Directory, "the ISO 27000 series of standards have been specifically reserved by ISO for information security matters. This, of course, aligns with a number of other topics, including ISO 9000 (quality management) and ISO 14000 (environmental management)."[18] These standards are relevant to all organizations and will serve as reasonable guidance for organizations wishing to mitigate risk while engaging global commerce. ISO standards are generally easy to understand and adaptable for more customized approaches. They are typically recognized and supported by a number of nations where similar or more particular national standards (United Kingdom, United States, etc.) may be resisted.

Technical controls are the most effective method to protect information and secure a computing environment. Physical controls include multilayered access authentication supplemented by exception reporting with video/audio and credential logging data. Administrative

[17]For a collection of food safety resources and training programs, visit the website for AIB International Food Defense Resource Center: www.aibonline.org/.
[18]The ISO 27000 Directory, "An Introduction to ISO 27001, ISO 27002 ... ISO 27008."

controls include the development and documentation of policies, standards, processes, procedures, and training. Once again a people, process, and technology approach protects both people and assets.

Good protection practices may likely converge as hybrid benchmarks replace many traditional physical and logical controls to improve interoperable asset protection. Stakeholders expect protection of their assets. Failure is more likely when organizations do not understand that both physical and logical protections are necessary or require coordination. Our ability to implement reasonable protection for sustainable and continuous incremental improvement remains to be seen.

Discussion Exercises

1. Identify surveys either completed or planned for your organization to determine how clients value your services.
2. List the security regulatory requirements for your company and rank them for compliance:
   A. Met (green)
   B. Work in progress (orange)
   C. Not resourced (red)
   Note planned mitigation time frames for any unattended risk. Identify programs or projects by name with relevant capital or annual expense. Enumerate any benefits other than compliance.

Additional Information and Resources

1. Professional associations and societies, Weddle's Association Directory: http://www.weddles.com/associations/index.cfm.
2. Association of Certified Fraud Examiners (ACFE): http://www.acfe.com/.
3. ASIS International: http://www.asisonline.org/.
4. International Security Management Association (ISMA): https://isma.com/.
5. The National Retail Federation, Preliminary results from the 2007 National Retail Security Survey: www.nrf.com/modules.php?name = News&op = viewlive&sp_id = 318.
6. The ISO 27000 Directory: http://www.27000.org/iso-27001.htm.
7. National Association of Regulatory Utility Commissioners (NARUC), Global Regulatory Network (GRN): *http://www.globalregulatory network.org.*
8. The Security Executive Council: https://www.securityexecutivecouncil.com/.

●●●

Well-crafted surveys enable communication of high-value information discreetly or anonymously to advance inquiries and performance. Professional associations and peer institutions can share state-of-the-art information with or without attribution. Benchmarking ensures that year-to-year issues, solutions, and measures are not lost to posterity.

The Requestor case study presented in this chapter was an actual benchmark case. All the recommendations were approved in the summer of 2008. Early results included hiring 16 LP professionals, eliminating $29 million in security officer expense, and improvement of both robbery and burglary risk, which decreased by 23 and 38 percent, respectively, per 1,000 stores.

CHAPTER 7

Governance for Sustainability

The rights, privileges, and protections of many stakeholder communities and built to last institutions stem from compacts and social contracts that govern conduct. Often the rights of individuals are tempered to ensure the viability of the host. Core values and guiding principles are seminal to establishing alliances, codes, guidelines, laws, policies, standards, and even performance objectives. From a compliance point of view, they allow us to inspect what we expect, hold each other accountable, and provide a foundation for cooperative accomplishment of needs and aspirations.

●●●

"... The problem is to find a form of association which will defend and protect with the whole common force the person and goods of each associate, and in which each, while uniting himself with all, may still obey himself alone, and remain as free as before. This is the fundamental problem of which the Social Contract provides the solution....

... The passage from the state of nature to the civil state produces a very remarkable change in man, by substituting justice for instinct in his conduct, and giving his actions the morality they had formerly lacked. Then only, when the voice of duty takes the place of physical impulses and right of appetite, does man, who so far had considered only himself, find that he is forced to act on different principles, and to consult his reason before listening to his inclinations. Although, in this state, he deprives himself of some advantages which he got from nature, he gains in return others so great, his faculties are so stimulated and developed, his ideas so extended, his feelings so ennobled, and his whole soul so uplifted, that, did not the abuses of this new condition often degrade him below that which he left, he would be bound to bless continually the happy moment which took him from it forever, and, instead of a stupid and unimaginative animal, made him an intelligent being and a man....

... But when the whole people decrees for the whole people, it is considering only itself; and if a relation is then formed, it is between two aspects of the entire object, without there being any division of the whole. In that case the matter about which the decree is made is, like the decreeing will, general. This act is what I call a law...."[1]

---

[1]Rousseau, *The Social Contract.*

These lofty words are the ruminations of Jean Jacques Rousseau, French Enlightenment philosopher. Rousseau's social contract was an idealistic compact among people envisioning the rule of law. The social contract enables the individual to pledge allegiance to a group, organization, or government with implicit understanding of duties and benefits. Governance for our purposes is more than mere "action or manner of governing"; it is the complicit agreement that we abide by certain principles and values that guide our conduct.[2] The philosophers of the Enlightenment aspired to modern democratic ideals. Patriots overthrew monarchies at their own peril to make it so. The social contract is an agreement for governance approved by the people. It is a conditional offer to enjoy the benefits of the community when one abides by rules, laws, and regulations.

Good security practices are similarly embedded in modern institutions as policies, standards, and guidelines with the beneficial objectives of protecting people, assets, and critical processes. Community security requires governance. Identities must be known and authorized activity must be licensed. Conduct is not necessarily monitored, but misbehavior that is potentially injurious to people or assets is subject to sanction. In the Aboriginal world this could mean physical punishment and banishment from the tribe. In the public sector we are subject to prosecution for offenses and omissions contrary to the law of the land. In business and other institutions we are held accountable for policy and legal breaches with personnel action up to and including termination, forfeiture of benefits, and referral to the courts for civil or criminal sanctions.

At Starbucks, governance begins with core values and principles that enable the mission "To inspire and nurture the human spirit—one person, one cup, and one neighborhood at a time." The Starbucks *Standards of Business Conduct* sets the tone for required behaviors and reporting duties.[3]

---

[2]*Oxford Pocket Dictionary of Current English*, 2nd ed., s.v. "governance."
[3]Starbucks Corporation, "Standards of Business Conduct."

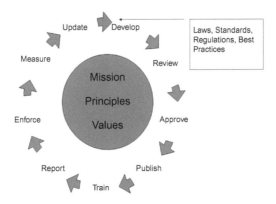

Figure 7.1 Policy Governance Lifecycle. © Crime Prevention Associates. All rights reserved.

Fundamentally, for Starbucks, ethical conduct and doing what's right spring from the core values of the culture and guiding principles. Legal requirements and standards are embedded in context.

Today, many companies have established compliance departments situated under a designated compliance officer to educate the community on ethical conduct and reporting requirements ranging from conflicts of interest to securities law questions. They typically coordinate all channel exception reporting for investigative follow-up and report regularly to leadership and the board of directors.

Policy governance teams may also play a role. Formal governance typically serves as an adjunct to ensure compliance efforts are supported with policy, procedure, and guideline resources that are catalogued for version control. Cross-functional efforts can include Legal, Human Resources, Information Technology, Finance, and Security support, with key operations representation. Like other cross-functional endeavors, sponsorship by influential officers like the general counsel, chief financial officer, and/or executive vice president of human resources can prove ideal. Enduring brand reputation protection requires the guardrails of a perpetual governance lifecycle. See Figure 7.1.

Laws, standards, regulations, and best practices guide development of governance tools. Review by a relevant cross-functional leadership group enables consideration by a wide audience, not only for approval but also to galvanize resources for implementation and maintenance including publication, training, audit reporting, and enforcement. Periodic reviews are necessary to update the tools to ensure compliance.

Good governance can require more than legal and regulatory compliance. Success or failure may be qualified by the mission, principles, and values that serve the greater good of the community. Cicero expressed the notion admirably: *Salus populi suprema est lex.* The good of the people is the chief law.[4]

Ethical conduct and responsible behavior are informed by cultural or community values even when circumstances not yet governed by law or policy evolve, such as ensuring medical benefits for persons afflicted by HIV, enabling all noncritical personnel to go home to their families with pay following 9/11, or supporting community members after a disaster. The members of the organization pick up ethical DNA by osmosis when integrity is nonnegotiable, demonstrated by leadership, and required of all stakeholders.

Open forums, town halls, and multichannel incident reporting (including anonymous options) can keep an organization honest when management intends to listen in earnest. Partners both applaud and challenge leadership on business decisions in the context of the culture. Input is encouraged in word and practice. The phrase "this is (or isn't) Starbucks" is used by passionate stakeholders from the newest partner to the chairman of the board.

It's not enough to adopt policy without attending it throughout its lifecycle. Nor can institutions afford disingenuous leaders. We have seen the consequences of words without practice. You may recall this attribution (summarized by the *New York Times*) to Kenneth Lay, chairman and CEO of Enron, after the Enron Code of Ethics manual surfaced on the Internet shortly following the company's fall from grace:

"We want to be proud of Enron and to know that it enjoys a reputation for fairness and honesty and that it is respected," Mr. Lay wrote in the manual's foreword. "Gaining such respect is one aim of our advertising and public relations activities, but no matter how effective they may be, Enron's reputation finally depends on its people, on you and me. Let's keep that reputation high."[5]

---

[4]The expression comes from *de Legibus* (On the Laws) a dialogue thought to have been written sometime during the first century B.C. by Marcus Tullius Cicero.
[5]Zeller, "The Nation; The Tao of Enron."

Ethical leadership is only one part of the recipe to warranty your organization's brand reputation. Ethical stakeholder engagement is another. Exception reporting must be encouraged and celebrated throughout the organization. Engaged stakeholders can balance risks including unethical leadership. Enron failed on multiple levels, including its too close relationship with its outside consultant and auditor, Arthur Andersen. Lessons learned may help us to not repeat similar failures.

The Ethics Resource Center developed a list of ten recommendations for companies that wish to avoid becoming the next Enron:

1. Examine your ethical climate and put safeguards in place
2. Don't just print, post, and pray
3. Build a robust ethics infrastructure that is self-sustaining
4. Publicly commit to being an ethical organization
5. Separate auditing from consulting functions
6. Talk with employees at all levels . . . often!
7. Build ethical conduct into corporate systems
8. Establish an Ethics Committee to constantly keep the seven main provisions of the Federal Sentencing Guidelines of 1991 in mind
9. Choose to live your corporate values
10. Keep the lines of communication open[6]

Live your values. If you are lucky you have sought employment with an organization that shares your ethical compass. If you are building your own small business, don't leave your mission, principles, and values statements to the future when you've "made it." This very exercise may enable your success, attracting talent and customers along the way. Research suggests ethical conduct pays. The United Kingdom's Institute of Business Ethics reported a strong correlation between business ethics and financial performance:

> The research is the most thorough study ever carried out in the United Kingdom of the relationship between business ethics and business performance in large companies. Using four indicators of business success economic value added (EVA), market value added (MVA), price/earnings ratio volatility (P/E ratio), and return on capital employed (ROCE)—it compared two groups of companies: those with a demonstrable commitment to ethical behavior through having a published code of business

[6]Gilman et al., "Ten Things You Can Do to Avoid Being the Next Enron."

ethics, and those without. Their performances were then analyzed over the five years between 1997 and 2001. On three of the four indicators (EVA, MVA, P/E), the companies with codes were clearly superior, and on ROCE the results were less clear but supported the overall trend.

- On Economic Value Added, the sample of companies with codes out-performed those without over a four-year period.
- On Market Value Added, the performance gap was even more marked.
- On Price/Earnings Ratio, the more demonstrable ethical companies showed far less volatility than the remainder.
- On Return on Capital Employed, companies with codes underper-formed those without between 1997 and 1999. Between 1999 and 2001, however, the trend was reversed, and ethical companies were clearly superior performers.[7]

Our building blocks for global security will increasingly rely on ethical, self-governing individuals and institutions that address their own risks and those of their neighbors.

We come together in simple social contracts and alliances looking to achieve common goals. More complex arrangements are required for multinational treaties including mutual assistance, defense, or trade. All will have security implications. Our conduct enables our relative pros-perity but brings other responsibilities. If we are to be resilient and capa-ble for the long term, we must take the view that stakeholder safety and security depend on continuous vigilance guided by our values.

Discussion Exercises

1. Give examples of good organizational conduct governed by mission, values, and principles that were rewarded with stakeholder valuation.
2. Give examples of poor organizational conduct contrary to mission, values, and principles that were penalized by stakeholders and/or a governing regulatory agency.

Additional Information and Resources

1. Cornell University's Policy Development Forum: http://www.sce.cor-nell.edu/exec/programs.php?v = 12187&s = Overview.
2. Institute of Business Ethics (IBE): http://www.ibe.org.uk/.
3. The Ethics Resource Center (ERC): http://www.ethics.org/.
4. The Centre for International Governance Innovation (CIGI): http://www.cigionline.org.

[7]Webley and More, "Does Business Ethics Pay?"

●●●

... Rousseau's concept of social contracts has since evolved to other codes of conduct. The principles of ethical behavior and organizational governance, often left to regulatory agencies and the courts when leadership and stakeholders fail, will be re-enforced. The current global turmoil in the banking and finance community strikes a familiar chord. Kenneth Lay, founder and former chairman of the board for Enron, and Jeffrey Skilling, the former chief executive officer of Enron, were convicted on multiple counts of fraud and conspiracy.[8] Those names, synonymous with self interest and entitlement, will be replaced by others. Bernard Lawrence "Bernie" Madoff is likely to be the new benchmark after pleading guilty to his multibillion "Ponzi" investment scheme in 2009. Regulators once again appear to have slept at the switch. Organizations that monitor ongoing risk and evolving international regulatory requirements within their own moral compass may continue to survive and thrive if rules-based behaviors are effectively audited and enforced.

---

[8]Shaheen Pasha and Jessica Seid, "Lay and Skilling's Day of Reckoning," *CNN Money.* May 25, 2006. money.cnn.com/2006/05/25/news/newsmakers/enron_verdict/index.htm?cnn = yes.

CHAPTER 8

Resilience

Resilience: 1: the capability of a strained body to recover its size and shape after deformation caused especially by compressive stress; 2: an ability to recover from or adjust easily to misfortune or change.[1]

Our efforts to elude catastrophic risk will always be tested by man-made acts, omissions, and the forces of nature. Our responsibility to continuously improve our mitigation and recovery capability remains achievable with common purpose. Long-term planning, periodic programming reviews, and preparedness pay dividends when communities demonstrate their values before, during, and after an event.

●●● ————————————————————————————————————

"... At first, the ocean pulled back. It was as if somewhere way out at sea a god pulled a giant plug on the bathtub. The water was sucked backwards, leaving only a muddy potholed ground, full of flopping fish and small holes of water.... They walked out and looked at the new landscape ... newly created children's pools just perfect for jumping in. They turned their backs to the distance. And yet others slept on the beach, taking in the cool and pleasant morning air....

... Many locals stood up at the retaining wall in awe, looking at their backyard sea of water that was no more. But they knew the power of the ocean, and like a man who had once been bit by a snake, were fearful to get any closer.... But then we saw the wall ... way out at sea.... If you blinked your eyes, it changed positions really fast.... For a few seconds, everyone was mesmerized by the wall and the sound. And then, with a snap of a finger, hundreds were popped out of their hypnosis—and people started to walk. Fast. And then run. And soon, everyone started to scream, "Get up on the wall!"....

... Some people stumbled. Some held their ground or were swept with the water towards the wall. People sputtered and coughed. The water spilled over the road. Some people went down—and most were in shock to have seen such a thing happen. But that was only the beginning. And while many people were able to stand back up again, bruised and battered, or having had all of their clothing ripped off by such a fast and switch wave, it wasn't over....

---

[1] *Merriam-Webster Online Dictionary*, s.v. "resilience."

... The second—and most deadly—swell came. And this one was the life taking swell. Larger, fiercer, taller by ten feet—this one just came so strongly—and pushed everything in its path towards the town. People were but leaves going under. This swell pushed all of the two hundred cars on the beach forward. It pushed hundreds of parked motorcycles and trucks. It pushed over the two buses parked in front of the dive shop, waiting to take divers collected from local hotels out to their morning dive.... .

... People at the Starbucks went screaming madly. In ten seconds, every piece of coffee equipment, chair, table, and bags of coffee were washed away. The only thing remaining were the lights hanging from the second story ceiling... . And the whole while, the morning sunshine warmed the day... ."[2]

What residents and tourists of the small town of Phuket, Thailand, experienced on the morning of December 26, 2004 was felt in communities across Thailand, Indonesia, Sri Lanka, India, and more. The devastation, triggered by a 9.3 magnitude earthquake off Sumatra, included 230,000 deaths across 13 countries, quickly becoming one of the deadliest natural disasters in known history.[3] How can communities that are virtually wiped out be resilient enough to bounce back?

Resilience was more of a hope than an expectation on December 27, 2004. The plight of these people prompted a widespread humanitarian response. Donations from the worldwide community are thought to number in the billions of dollars.

In addition to the horrific loss of life and injuries, key community infrastructure components including housing, roads, bridges, hospitals, schools, and community buildings were washed away or badly damaged. Survival was the first order of business. Assurance of safe drinking water, health care, and temporary housing were required. The enormity of the event prompted comprehensive planning improvements for more robust infrastructure. Both placement and construction of public utilities ranging from drinking water systems to tsunami warning capability were implemented.

---

[2] Story excerpted from "Nature's Ugly Hand: What We Saw," by Rick Von Feldt. © Rick Von Feldt. All rights reserved. Used with permission.
[3] *NBC News Photo Blog*, "Remembering the 2004 Indian Ocean Tsunami."

The security implications for disaster are many. If and when governance breaks down, criminal activity accelerates. Even when aid arrives, criminal diversion or perceived distribution inequities may result in civil disobedience or riots. The relative nimbleness and security of supply chains will be challenged as transportation infrastructure is damaged and diversion escalates.

Hurricane Katrina was similarly instructive. It demonstrated the importance of both infrastructure and evacuation preparedness in 2005 when the Category 3 hurricane swept over the Gulf of Mexico to Southeastern Louisiana and Mississippi, devastating many communities including New Orleans. Despite weeks of risk warnings, levee breeches and flood wall failures left much of the city of New Orleans underwater. Damages resulted in more than 1,800 deaths and property losses estimated at $81 billion.[4]

Scenes of devastation with enormous casualties have surprised all who expected the world to be better prepared post-9/11. Perhaps more alarmingly, many of our remaining public safety hazards remain relatively unaddressed by public policy—from eroding levee and transportation infrastructure to petrochemical industrial adjacencies within large population centers. Even if we set the risk of terrorism aside, our presumptive mentality that aging infrastructure does not require routine maintenance, replacement, improvement, or relocation exacerbates the certainty of preventable or mitigatable disasters. Accidents, extreme weather conditions, and seismic events alone will take their toll.

8.1 RESPONSIBILITY ENSURES RESILIENCE

We must address our own sense of entitlement to live with unnecessary risk as a prerequisite for any discussion of resilience. Our collective presumption of rights and privileges without responsibility results in poor public policy, unnecessary community hazards, and diminished resources to improve sustainability. In his 1994 book, *The Spirit of Community,* former Brookings scholar, White House advisor, and well-known sociologist Amitai Etzioni asserts that "claiming rights without assuming responsibilities is unethical and illogical."[5] National printing presses cannot produce currency in perpetuity to

---

[4]*The Weather Channel*, "Katrina's Statistics Tell Story."
[5]Etzioni, *The Spirit of Community.*

cover the avoidable losses and costs generated by unethical or ineffective leadership aided and abetted by an absentee citizenry. Etzioni also explains:

"Presidents ... backed up by Congress ... suggested that ever-increasing economic growth would pay for government services and taxpayers would be expected to shell out less—implying that Americans could have their cake and eat it too."

That notion seems to be shared by the entitled and the privileged around the globe.

Our responsibility to achieve resilience requires compensatory innovation and investment. Responsible leaders recognize early on that entitlement borne of success can be a hurdle for sustainability. For Howard Schultz, entitlement was always a risk. He constantly calls for reexamination for incremental engagement, reinvestment, and reinvention to earn the trust and loyalty of stakeholders. Conditions change. Organizations must maintain their relevancy.

Starbucks recognized that the "coffee, culture, and community" experience is globally interdependent. C.A.F.E. (coffee and farmer equity) practices provided incentives tied to coffee quality to enable both farmer economic viability and crop sustainability. Starbucks knew that these commitments could be repeated in hundreds of global communities. Incremental agronomy improvements translated to premium coffee prices and commitments for community improvements including clinics, schools, potable water resources, and sanitation improvements. Starbucks provides an annual public report on its responsibility initiatives, which include community activism, ethical sourcing, and monitoring and reducing its environmental footprint.[6]

Our security depends on the security of those around us and those we depend on from afar. Resilience does not trickle down. It is built from the foundation up with shared values and responsibilities. Strong communities that have thoughtfully planned for risk conditions and are capable of mutual assistance are better situated for global resilience. Honest leadership and transparent discussion of risk persuade us that population centers; industrial production; and public utilities, transportation, and

---

[6]Starbucks Corporation, "Responsibility."

dependent supply chains require rethinking, reinvestment, reinvention, and possible relocation. Our incremental security improvement opportunities are many, beginning with risk awareness and responsible mitigation. Qualified privileges will include credentialed access governed by principles and values.

Regulation of high-risk behavior is required to prevent or mitigate devastating reoccurrences of outcomes that we cannot afford to repeat. Flood plain, coastal, and seismic development occupancy policies need rethinking. Zoning and building codes have to reflect recorded risk. Disaster readiness, from "shelter-in-place" to evacuation, dictates personal and organizational commitment for awareness, training, kit building, and special equipment needs. Resources are finite. Ideally they must be prioritized for prevention and loss avoidance and curtailed for losses that are exacerbated by contributory negligence. Short-term security planning will attempt to identify all hazards and existing mitigations in order to prioritize solution programming. Short-term planning will periodically recur and inform long-term and ongoing risk management goals. For example, see the diagram excerpted from ISO 28001 (Security Management Systems for the Supply Chain) in Figure 8.1.

Supply chain threat scenarios will include all manmade accidents and criminal acts from adulteration to diversion and theft, as well as natural catastrophes that threaten goods in transit, at rest, or in the manufacturing process. Long-term security and safety goals typically will be required with multiyear strategic planning. Our ability to share measures of success and failure, short of inappropriately revealing core proprietary or secret information, will inform others. Security should not be viewed solely as a risk avoidance operation. It must enable the community to take reasonable risks based on sober calculation of benefits with a plausible mitigation strategy. It is an instrument to demonstrate organizational vision and values with responsible conduct to earn reputation.

8.2 RESILIENCE REQUIRES PREPAREDNESS

Manmade catastrophes and naturally occurring phenomena, from contagion to seismic or severe weather events, have endangered us since the dawn of civilization. Our anxiety for a range of hazards is palpable. The so-called "death of distance," a phrase coined by Frances

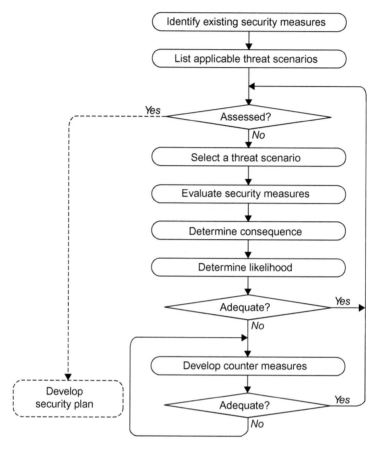

Figure 8.1 Continuous Security Risk Assessment. This excerpt is taken from ISO 28001:2007, Figure B-1 on page 19, with the permission of ANSI on behalf of ISO. © ISO 2013 — All rights reserved.

Cairncross to describe the globe-shrinking effect of instantaneous communications, reminds us of every prevention or mitigation miss.[7]

We began this millennium with high anxiety related to the Y2K time code ambiguity. Many surmised that date-related machine processing would fail on January 1, 2000. Widespread utility grid and critical systems issues were anticipated. First responder teams were on alert throughout the world. Yet relatively little disruption occurred thanks to the mitigation efforts of program managers and their developers. It was not until 2001 that the world was shaken by multiple influencing

[7]Cairncross, *The Death of Distance.*

events. On January 26, 2001, the Gujarat region of India and a portion of eastern Pakistan were devastated by an estimated 7.6 + magnitude earthquake. Estimated deaths exceeded 20,000. Injuries topped 167,000 with more than a million homes destroyed. "Pandemic Threat Posed by Avian Influenza Viruses" was also published.[8] The research findings by Taisuke Horimoto and Yoshihiro Kawaoka warned of similarities between H5N1 and the Spanish influenza H1N1 that claimed 20 million victims worldwide in 1918 and 1919.

Later in 2001, on September 11, all eyes turned to the United States when primetime news footage showed the consequences of Osama Bin Laden's long-standing threat: 2,974 victims and 19 suicide terrorists died with the destruction of the World Trade Center's twin towers in New York, and the Pentagon sustained heavy damage.

Identity theft and fraud kept pace with network expansion, enabling subjects of interest (including the 9/11 hijackers) to travel with impunity under alias credentials. Identity theft topped the US Federal Trade Commission's consumer complaints in 2001. Enron, the $64 billion energy trading giant, declared bankruptcy. Failed fraud detection oversight cost the brand and all its stakeholders.

In October 2001, the Amerithrax anthrax attacks reminded the United States that domestic terrorism can be just as effectively disruptive as any imported variety. 2001 was also the last time the FDA visited a Blakely, Georgia, food manufacturing facility that later distributed salmonella-laced product to unsuspecting consumers with fatal results. Harry Markopoulos, a Certified Fraud Examiner, made his way for the second time to the US Securities and Exchange Commission (SEC) with incontrovertible proof of the largest Ponzi scheme in history. They did not heed his warning.

8.3 LEARNING OUR WAY

The heroic recovery efforts of 2001 were well documented. The events of that year influenced crisis response and business continuity. Multiple sectors reshaped precautionary government and nongovernmental organization advisories to reach diverse global audiences:

[8]Horimoto and Kawaoka, "Pandemic Threat Posed by Avian Influenza Viruses."

1. Evacuation and shelter-in-place guidelines
2. Procedures for mail handling and identifying or reporting suspicious packages
3. Security guidelines including facility access control and suspicion reporting
4. Travel guidelines, restrictions, and tips
5. All-channel risk reporting and status update communications protocol

The realization that all-hazards protection was required became obvious as risk-related compliance legislation was passed in every country around the world. Resulting board-level risk brought the protection portfolio into the light. Governments began to understand that arguably 90 percent of critical infrastructure is in the private-sector domain. They also learned that response to global catastrophe required all hands, including nongovernmental organizations (NGOs).

8.4 THE VALUE OPPORTUNITY

The dots are there for protection professionals and others to connect. Current and evolving risk resilience requires courageous cross-functional leadership and systematic methodologies that will transcend any one group. Brand reputation in any sector will continue to be earned by those who can take a hit and bounce back. There is much work to do before, during, and after the next disasters of consequence—and there are fewer resources.

High-morbidity pandemics are still on the horizon. Networks remain both the target and the means for multinational organized crime including theft, fraud, and terror. Criminals, inside and out, continue to exploit the soft targets around the world. Critical infrastructure, including intelligence and first responder agencies, are still uncomfortably vulnerable. More than ever, supply chain and critical process management are required for both proprietary and critical dependency environments. Threat appreciation, exception detection, and response preparedness must be improved.

The failures of persuasive risk detection, compliance, and effective mitigation have left us with unnecessary injury, death, damage, loss, and deficits worldwide. Confidence has been measured at an all-time

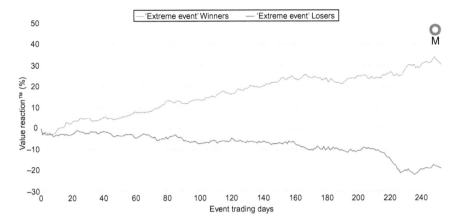

low since the Great Depression. Counterintuitively, the resultant downsizing, rightsizing, and re engineering may be a gift—if and when we redeploy more intelligent, nimble, cross-functional, and return-on-investment capable protection elements. Good and best practices will continue to evolve from risk intelligence linked with integrated mitigation innovation and performance.

The data is in. Brand reputation is performance dependent. Stakeholders can no longer afford only heroic efforts after the fact. They expect us to prevent and mitigate while navigating both compliance and emerging risk. Cross-functional talent, tools, and training are required to prepare for and weather the storm. Mass casualty events of the recent past inform future stakeholder expectations and valuation.

In their 2006 report, *Protecting Value in the Face of Mass Fatality Events,* Doctors Rory Knight and Deborah Pretty analyzed shareholder value impacts for a wide range of firms following mass casualty events including aviation disasters, fires and explosions, terrorist attacks, and natural catastrophes. Figure 8.2 implies that the ability to manage a mass-fatality event (i.e., winners) is even more impressive to investors, and the *inability* to manage such an event (i.e., losers) is even more disappointing than in less tragic corporate crises. The Knight and Pretty analysis concluded that:

1. Mass casualty events have double the impact on shareholder value than corporate catastrophes in general.
2. The market makes a rapid judgment on whether it expects reputation to be damaged or enhanced by a crisis. However, shocking news takes time to be digested and, in the case of mass fatality events, the multiplier effect on value takes, on the average, 100 trading days to emerge prominently.
3. As with non-fatal reputation crises for firms, the key determinant of value recovery relates to the ability of senior management to demonstrate strong leadership and to communicate at all times with honesty and transparency.
4. For mass casualty events particularly, the sensitivity and compassion with which the chief executive responds to victims' families and the logistical care and efficiency with which response teams carry out their work is paramount. There is a forty percent value premium associated with the engagement of such specialist services.
5. Irrespective of whose responsibility is the cause of the mass casualty event, a sensitive managerial response is critical to the sustaining and creation of shareholder value.[9]

Bruce Blythe of Crisis Management International helps make the persuasive case for the human side of crisis response, recovery, and preparedness.[10] He notes that preparedness will be the "next wave" of corporate compliance, citing US Public Law 110-53, the international draft standard ISO/PAS 22399, and Standard and Poor's enterprise risk management (ERM) rating initiative of 2009 that will likely affect institutional creditworthiness.[11]

Crisis Management International and the Alfred P. Sloan Foundation partnered in a June 2008 survey that added relevance. According to a webinar Blythe held after the survey was completed:

1. Nearly all companies have exposure to disaster prone areas with 77 percent experiencing an emergency in the past five years.
2. Larger companies, especially within the Department of Homeland Security's critical infrastructure industries, are most well prepared.
3. The human side of crisis was the least prepared aspect of planning.[12]

[9] Knight and Pretty, *Protecting Value in the Face of Mass Fatality Events.*
[10] Blythe, *Blindsided.*
[11] Standard and Poor's Rating Services, "Enterprise Risk Management."
[12] Blythe, "Webinar: The Human Side of Business Continuity and Crisis Management."

Communities that invest for the protection of people, assets, and critical processes and reserve specialist services before, during, and after an event will most likely be resilient. The ability to perceive risk, plan infrastructure investment, and effectively orchestrate response will enhance our safety and economic security.

8.5 EVOLVING INDIVIDUAL AND ORGANIZATIONAL BEHAVIOR

How do we rise from our baseline needs to not only be self-actualized but resilient on this high-risk planet? Michael Shermer, the publisher of *Skeptic Magazine,* pondered "the purpose pyramid."[13] He combined Abraham Maslow's hierarchy of needs and Peter Singer's expanding circle of sentiments to depict the 1.5 million years of evolution that were necessary to develop from individual protection interest to family, extended family, the community, society, species, and biosphere interests. See Figure 8.3.

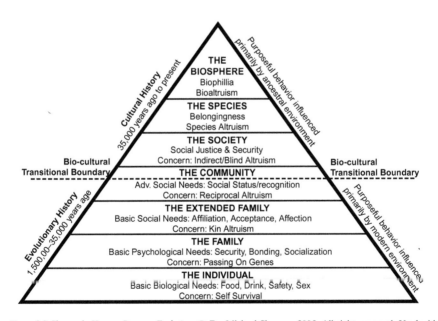

Figure 8.3 Shermer's Human Purpose Evolution. © Dr. Michael Shermer, 2005. All rights reserved. Used with permission.

---

[13]Shermer, "The Soul of Science."

Shermer cites Thomas Jefferson and scientific research to support his notion that our pro-social behavior makes us feel good. Feeling good about oneself while protecting interests may be the nexus for organizational and community engagement to ensure loyalty and productivity from the best and the brightest. Community and global resilience may be the higher purpose required to replace the individual and organizational greed we have witnessed at the turn of this millennium.

Shermer makes it clear that the value opportunity occurs well before a catastrophic event. Ethical for-profit organizations are leading the way for understanding the sustainable opportunities that are borne with public sector and NGO alliances to reinvest and trade with our most fragile interdependent communities.

Discussion Exercises

1. Select any major global natural catastrophe in the past five years and discuss the role of infrastructure readiness or lack thereof in casualty and damage impacts. Assess recovery efforts and the relative resilience improvements on a scale of 1 to 10.
2. Cite an example of an inadequate response to product-related injuries or deaths that cost a multinational corporation reputational damage, sales, and market value. Identify a competitor that improved market share after a catastrophe.

Additional Information and Resources

1. Stephen Flynn's *The Edge of Disaster*. Published in 2007 by Random House.
2. Business Resilience Certification Consortium International (BRCCI): www.brcci.org/index.htm.
3. International Federation of Red Cross and Red Crescent Societies for emergency relief operations: http://www.ifrc.org/en/get-involved/donate/.
4. ISO/PAS 22399:2007 Societal security - Guideline for incident preparedness and operational continuity management: www.iso.org/iso/catalogue_detail.htm?csnumber = 50295.
5. National Fire Protection Association's NFPA 1600 standard on disaster/emergency management and business continuity programs: http://www.nfpa.org/catalog/product.asp?pid = 160013.
6. Title IX of US Public Law 110-530—August 3, 2007 – Implementing Recommendations of the 9/11 Commission Act of 2007: http://www.gpo.gov/fdsys/pkg/PLAW-110publ53/pdf/PLAW-110publ53.pdf.
7. Standard and Poor's enterprise risk management (ERM) rating initiative of 2009: www.standardandpoors.com/ratings/erm/en/us/.

●●●

"Focusing on six key areas—water and sanitation, psychosocial support, health, shelter, livelihoods, and disaster preparedness—the Tsunami Recovery Program has supported more than 80 relief and recovery projects in 10 countries. Because of the generosity of donors, beneficiaries received more than immediate relief—they received resources, services and training that will help them thrive for years to come.

"[In 2009, five years after the tsunami], villages teem[ed] with activity, classrooms [we]re full of students, and marketplaces [we]re alive with business ... survivors [we]re embracing a brighter future."[14]

Starbucks Coffee earmarked more than one million dollars to support the recovery. Response to Katrina in the United States brought a pledge of $5 million and numerous stakeholder lead projects through 2008.

A portion of the net proceeds from this book will be donated in perpetuity to the International Federation of Red Cross and Red Crescent Societies for emergency relief operations.

---

[14]The American Red Cross, "Tsunami Recovery Program: Five-Year Report."

HOW DO WE MAKE SURE THIS NEVER HAPPENS AGAIN, GLOBALLY?

●●●

Moments earlier Nancy Kent had called to see if I "had a few minutes for Howard." I invariably did. On my way upstairs, I clicked off three situations of consequence in my own head that might be of interest and pondered the likelihood of a wild card issue that Howard might introduce.

Howard Schultz is one of the most strategic thinkers that I have met. He is certainly the most empathetic leader I have ever known. His questions nearly always cut to the core of an issue and seldom were irrelevant or uncivil. I have had the occasion to see him in action for over a decade on high consequence—if not life and death—issues.

Howard's concern was always for those at risk. He characteristically calculated the human predicament with heartfelt empathy. I had seen this careworn look before in the aftermath of the Georgetown homicides, the Nisqually earthquake, 9/11, SARS, the Sumatra Tsunami, and Katrina. His dark eyes were sincere and emotional when he asked, "How do we make sure this never happens again . . . globally?"

We both understood that the concept of 100 percent prevention was hypothetically unreachable with finite protection resources. Our conversations regarding our choices and priorities for mitigation were nevertheless reality checks for priorities within the mission guardrails.

At Starbucks, building coffee stores was a primary focus. Yet much had been accomplished against a wide array of risks. Security investment had been informed by the hazards for sourcing and delivering the Starbucks experience around the world. Millions of dollars had been spent, and we saw results and return on investment. Significant inroads had been made for stakeholder protection; fraud detection; information and supply chain security; and the protection of people, assets, critical processes, and brand reputation while ensuring margin contribution.

Prioritized risk and informed mitigation produced measured if inelegant and unfinished results. Most importantly, cross-functional teams enabled a principled mission. That inspirational goal of lifting the human spirit, from remote coffee country elevations to hundreds of diverse global markets, was still within sight. Near catastrophic events had proven our ability to reprioritize, repurpose, and redirect.

A just-in-time protection approach remained programmable and flexible enough to effectively respond to world events, all-hazard intelligence, and regulatory compliance. Protection improvement is rarely perfected. It is ongoing and includes relevant reinvention and reconsolidation of security resources within organizations based on reassessment of evolving risks and mitigation opportunities. Priorities are reconsidered for new hazards without losing sight of those that have visited in the past. The principled approach always comes back to community, family, and self before institutional and global security can be perpetuated.

Since my undertaking this book, we have collectively witnessed assassinations, genocide, global recession, institutional and nation-state failures, looming pandemics, piracy, regional wars, resurgent crime and violence, seismic upheavals, storms of the century, terror threats, water and food shortages, and wild fires. Yet hope for change burns undeniably. It keeps all eyes glued on the American general elections and international financial reforms. Efforts to more effectively husband resources, influence improved health and environment, and innovate and revisit alliances for more effective safety and security resonate.

The themes of this book were formed with business colleagues, friends, and strangers all over the world. Our global travels were warmed by the hospitality and good will of many who voiced their concerns for improved public and private sector safety and security. Now is the time to take ownership for our future relative safety and prosperity as we assess the risk landscape, make a plan, and prepare our kit. Our collective determination to assist neighbors, distributed family members, and dependent communities will take us off our doorstep, through the neighborhood, and across borders for measurable risk mitigation.

Innovation will be the byword for better, more cost-effective, and greener solutions. Trust but verify will once again rein in unfettered market forces. Protection professionals can lead the way to regain the engagement required to restore institutional integrity.

This generation and its followers will be asked to rebuild infrastructure. We must be trained, equipped, and ready to serve ourselves and others. This will require elimination of unnecessary losses and fraud to pay the way. Our ability to influence responsible organizations and institutions including government to these ends will incrementally improve our resilience. We will rededicate ourselves to these purposes because we are motivated by the likely consequence of inaction.

Climate will still change. Pathogens will infect. Tectonic plates will shift. Criminal elements will threaten our lives and prosperity. Honest, hardworking people will continue to be victimized in varying degrees depending on their personal risk awareness and preparedness. Our resolve to advance community agendas and to recognize the risks, invest for mitigation, influence continuous improvement, and hold others accountable for acts and omissions that hazard our well-being will serve to prevent unnecessary loss and damage. Unnecessary recovery expense can be repurposed for infrastructure reinvestment and innovative problem solving.

There is always light in the darkest hour for those who are prepared. Winston Churchill offers timeless guidance for the value of leadership courage that should serve us well.

"During these crowded days of the political crisis, my pulse had not quickened at any moment. I took it all in as it came. But I cannot conceal from the reader of this truthful account that as I went to bed at about 3:00 a.m., I was conscious of a profound sense of relief. At last I had the authority to give directions over the whole scene. I felt as if I were walking with Destiny, and that all my past life had been but a preparation for this hour and this trial.... . My warnings over the last six years had been so numerous, so detailed and now were so terribly vindicated, that no one could gainsay me. I could not be reproached for either making the war or with want of preparation for it.... . Therefore, although impatient for the morning, I slept soundly and had no need for cheering dreams. Facts are better than dreams."[1]

---

[1]Churchill, *The Gathering Storm.*

Panic is not an option when influencing our communities. Leadership courage may be gained and advanced by sober assessment of exceptional risks. Properly integrated resources including people, process, and technology enable ROI-capable, just-in-time mitigation. Continuous improvement demands that knowledge-based innovation and good practices are measured and shared by an engaged, trustworthy people and asset protection community. Our collective efforts will make a difference at home, in our village or town, state or province, country or region, and across the globe. There is not a moment to lose.

Francis is a principal of Crime Prevention Associates and emeritus faculty of the Security Executive Council. He is a Certified Protection Professional (CPP), Certified Fraud Examiner (CFE), Community Emergency Responder, Food Defense Coordinator, and Coffee Master.

He is a seasoned all-hazards risk mitigation leader for multinational convenience, food and beverage, manufacturing, restaurant, retail, and supply chain operators. He has served as chief security officer for Starbucks Coffee, Hardees Food Systems, and Jerrico Inc. His expertise includes risk diligence, loss prevention, and mitigation systems design, as well as contribution analytics.

Francis was named one of the "25 Most Influential People in Security" in 2009 by *Security* magazine and was a *CSO* magazine 2007 Compass Award honoree.

He is also the critically acclaimed author of *The Manager's Violence Survival Guide* (1995) and *Loss Prevention through Crime Analysis* (1989).

About Elsevier's Security Executive Council Risk Management Portfolio

Elsevier's Security Executive Council Risk Management Portfolio is the voice of the security leader. It equips executives, practitioners, and educators with research-based, proven information and practical solutions for successful security and risk management programs. This portfolio covers topics in the areas of risk mitigation and assessment, ideation and implementation, and professional development. It brings trusted operational research, risk management advice, tactics, and tools to business professionals. Previously available only to the Security Executive Council community, this content—covering corporate security, enterprise crisis management, global IT security, and more—provides real-world solutions and "how-to" applications. This portfolio enables business and security executives, security practitioners, and educators to implement new physical and digital risk management strategies and build successful security and risk management programs.

Elsevier's Security Executive Council Risk Management Portfolio is a key part of the **Elsevier Risk Management & Security Collection**. The collection provides a complete portfolio of titles for the business executive, practitioner, and educator by bringing together the best imprints in risk management, security leadership, digital forensics, IT security, physical security, homeland security, and emergency management: Syngress, which provides cutting-edge computer and information security material; Butterworth-Heinemann, the premier security, risk management, homeland security, and disaster-preparedness publisher; and Anderson Publishing, a leader in criminal justice publishing for more than 40 years. These imprints, along with the addition of Security Executive Council content, bring the work of highly regarded authors into one prestigious, complete collection.

The Security Executive Council (www.securityexecutivecouncil.com) is a leading problem-solving research and services organization focused on helping businesses build value while improving their ability to effectively manage and mitigate risk. Drawing on the collective knowledge of a large community of successful security practitioners, experts, and strategic alliance partners, the Council develops strategy and insight and identifies proven practices that cannot be found anywhere else. Their research, services, and tools are focused on protecting people, brand, information, physical assets, and the bottom line.

Elsevier (www.elsevier.com) is an international multimedia publishing company that provides world-class information and innovative solutions tools. It is part of Reed Elsevier, a world-leading provider of professional information solutions in the science, medical, risk, legal, and business sectors.

REFERENCES

Armstrong III, Frank. "In a World of Madoffs, Remember What Reagan Said about Trust." *Forbes*. August 31, 2012. <http://www.forbes.com/sites/greatspeculations/2012/08/31/in-a-world-of-madoffs-remember-what-reagan-told-gorbachev-about-trust/>.

Association of Certified Fraud Examiners, Inc. (ACFE). "Report to the Nations on Occupational Fraud and Abuse: 2012 global Fraud Study." 2012. <http://www.acfe.com/uploadedFiles/ACFE_Website/Content/rttn/2012-report-to-Nations.pdf>.

Baribeau, Simone, and Ellen Nakashima. "11 Charged in Global Theft, Sale of 40 Million Card Numbers." *Washington Post*. August 6, 2008. <www.washingtonpost.com/wp-dyn/content/article/2008/08/05/AR2008080501859.html>.

Bernstein, Peter. *Against the Gods: The Remarkable Story of Risk*. New York: John Wiley and Sons, 1996.

Blades, Marleah. "No Size Fits All." *Security Technology Executive*. April 22, 2009. <http://www.securityinfowatch.com/article/10516188/no-size-fits-all>.

Blythe, Bruce. *Blindsided: A Manager's Guide to Catastrophic Incidents in the Workplace*. New York: Portfolio, 2002.

___. "Webinar: The Human Side of Business Continuity and Crisis Management." August 13, 2008. <www.cmiatl.com>.

Bridges, Sarah. "Retailer Target Branches Out Into Police Work." *The Washington Post*. January 29, 2006. <www.washingtonpost.com/wp-dyn/content/article/2006/01/28/AR2006012801268_pf.html>.

Cairncross, Frances. *The Death of Distance: How the Communications Revolution Will Change Our Lives*. Boston: Harvard Business School Press, 1997.

Campbell, George K. *Measures and Metrics in Corporate Security: Communicating Business Value*. Boston: The Security Executive Council, 2006.

Cateriniccia, Dan. "Companies Avoid Financial Penalties After Massive Computer Data Breaches." *Washington Post*. March 28, 2008. <www.washingtonpost.com/wp-dyn/content/article/2008/03/27/AR2008032703436.html>.

Chapman, Alan. "Abraham Maslow's Hierarchy of Needs Motivational Model." Businessballs. Accessed July 8, 2013. <www.businessballs.com/maslow.htm>.

Churchill, Winston. *The Gathering Storm*. Boston: Houghton Mifflin Company, 1948.

Clark, John P., and Richard C. Hollinger. *Theft by Employees in Work Organizations: Executive Summary*. Washington: National Institute of Justice, 1983.

Coenen, Tracy. "The True Cost of Fraud." *All Business*. January 24, 2008. <www.allbusiness.com/crime-law-enforcement-corrections/criminal-offenses-fraud/5222152-1.html>.

Collins, James C., and Jerry I. Porras. *Built to Last: Successful Habits of Visionary Companies*. New York: HarperBusiness, 1994.

Crow, Wayman, and James Bull. *Robbery Deterrence: An Applied Behavioral Science Demonstration*. La Jolla: Western Behavioral Sciences Institute, 1975.

D'Addario, Francis J. "ISO/PAS 28001 Enables Starbucks Coffee Company's Supply Chain Strategy." *ISO Focus*. July/August 2006. <www.iso.org/iso/livelinkgetfile-isocs?nodeId = 15006548>.

___. *The Manager's Violence Survival Guide*. Chapel Hill: Crime Prevention Associates, Inc, 1995.

D'Addario, Francis J., the National Crime Prevention Institute. *Loss Prevention through Crime Analysis*. Boston: Butterworth-Heinemann, 1989.

Daughton, Sandi. "Pinpointing Devastation if Seattle Fault Ruptures." *The Seattle Times*. February 20, 2005. <http://community.seattletimes.nwsource.com/archive/?date = 20050220&slug = earthquake20m>.

de Becker, Gavin. *The Gift of Fear: Survival Signals that Protect Us from Violence*. Boston: Little Brown and Company, 1997.

Diamond, Jared. *Collapse: How Societies Choose To Fail or Succeed*. New York: Viking Penguin, 2005.

Erickson, Rosemary. *Teenage Robbers: How and Why They Rob*. San Diego: Athena Research Corporation, August 2003. <http://athenaresearch.com/materials/prchs_trhwr.pdf>.

Ethisphere Institute. "World's Most Ethical Companies − Honorees." Accessed July 8, 2013. <http://ethisphere.com/worlds-most-ethical/wme-honorees/>.

Etzioni, Amitai. *The Spirit of Community: The Reinvention of American Society*. New York: Touchstone, 1994.

Federal Bureau of Investigation (FBI). "Crime Statistics 2007: The Preliminary Numbers." June 9, 2008. <http://www.hsdl.org/?view&did = 486603>.

___. "Minneapolis Division Director's Community Leadership Award Recipients." Accessed July 23, 2013. <http://www.fbi.gov/minneapolis/news-and-outreach/outreach/minneapolis-division-directors-community-leadership-award-recipients>.

Flynn, Stephen. *The Edge of Disaster*. New York: Random House, 2007.

Fortune Magazine. "100 Best Companies to Work For 2007." January 22, 2007. <money.cnn.com/magazines/fortune/bestcompanies/2007/full_list/>.

Frand, Rabbi Yissocher. "A Good Name Is Better than Good Oil." Accessed July 9, 2013. <http://www.hakhel.info/archivesShatnez/ShatnezDvarTorah.pdf>.

Gilman, Dr. Stuart, Patricia, Dr. Harned, Frank Navran, and Jerry Brown. "10 Things You Can Do to Avoid Being the Next Enron." Ethics Resource Center. May 29, 2009. <www.ethics.org/resource/ten-things-you-can-do-avoid-being-next-enron>.

Gladwell, Malcolm. *The Tipping Point: How Little Things Can Make A Big Difference*. New York: Little Brown, 2000.

Grannis, Kathy. "Retail Losses Hit $41.6 Billion Last Year, According to National Retail Security Survey." National Retail Federation. June 11, 2007. <www.nrf.com/modules.php?name = News&op = viewlive&sp_id = 318>.

Griffin, Joel. "Roundtable: Lessons Learned from Virginia Tech." *Security Info Watch*. April 19, 2013. <http://www.securityinfowatch.com/article/10703301/roundtable-lessons-learned-from-virginia-tech>.

Hansen, Ronald J. "Starbucks to Reopen after Slayings." *The Washington Times*. July 16, 1997. <www.highbeam.com/doc/1G1-56808315.html>.

Harter, James K., Frank L. Schmidt, and Corey L.M. Keyes. "Well-Being in the Workplace and Its Relationship to Business Outcomes." Gallup Research. 2003. <media.gallup.com/DOCUMENTS/whitePaper−Well-BeingInTheWorkplace.pdf>.

Horimoto, Taisuke, and Yoshihiro Kawaoka. "Pandemic Threat Posed by Avian Influenza Viruses." *Clinical Microbiology Reviews, 14*(no. 1). 2001. Available from http://dx.doi.org/10.1128/CMR.14.1.129-149.2001.

Isidore, Chris. "Consumer Confidence at Five-Year High." *CNN Money*. June 25, 2013. <http://money.cnn.com/2013/06/25/news/economy/consumer-confidence/index.html>.

Jenkins, Lynn. "Violence in the Workplace." *NIOSH Current Intelligence Bulletin, no. 57*. July 1996. <http://www.cdc.gov/niosh/docs/96-100/>.

Kirk, Jeremy. "Identity Fraud in the United States Reaches Highest Level in Three Years." *Computerworld*. February 20, 2013. <http://www.computerworld.com/s/article/9236999/Identity_fraud_in_US_reaches_highest_level_in_three_years>.

Knight, Rory, and Deborah Pretty. *Protecting Value in the Face of Mass Fatality Events*. London: Oxford Metrica, 2006. <http://oxfordmetrica.com/public/CMS/Files/601/04RepComKen.pdf>.

Leen, Jeff. "A Dance with Death (The Untold Story of the Starbucks Triple Homicide Investigation)." *Washington Post Magazine*. March 2, 2003.

Maslow, Abraham. *Motivation and Personality*. New York: Addison-Wesley, 1987.

Naím, Moisés. *Illicit: How Smugglers, Traffickers, and Copycats Are Hijacking the Global Economy*. New York: Anchor Books, 2005.

National Commission on Terrorist Attacks in the United States. "The 9/11 Commission Report." July 2004. <http://www.9-11commission.gov/report/911Report.pdf>.

NBC News Photo Blog. "Remembering the 2004 Indian Ocean Tsunami amid Destroyed Buildings." December 26, 2012. <http://photoblog.nbcnews.com/_news/2012/12/26/16163844-remembering-the-2004-indian-ocean-tsunami-amid-destroyed-buildings?lite>.

Occupational Safety and Health Administration (OSHA). *Recommendations for Workplace Violence Prevention Programs in Late-Night Retail Establishments*. 2009. <https://www.osha.gov/Publications/osha3153.pdf>.

Parrett, William G. *The Sentinel CEO: Perspectives on Security, Risk, and Leadership in a Post-9/11 World*. New Jersey: John Wiley and Sons Inc., 2007.

Paulson, Michael. "Starbucks Moves beyond Tragedy: DC Store Is Reopened after Three Killings in July." *Seattle Post Intelligencer*. February 20, 1998.

Rappleye Jr., Willard C. "Thrust and Counterthrust." *Conference Board Review*, 45(no. 1). 2008.

Reynolds, George. "ConAgra Estimates Peanut Butter Recall Will Cost $60m." *Food Production Daily*. February 20, 2007. <www.foodproductiondaily.com/Quality-Safety/ConAgra-estimates-peanut-butter-recall-will-cost-60m>.

Rigzone. "Boots and Coots." Accessed July 12, 2013. <www.rigzone.com/news/company.asp?comp_id = 448>.

Robinson, J.J. "Business Partners (Pose the) Greatest Security Threat." *Information Age*. June 20, 2008. <www.information-age.com/home/information-age-today/443066/business-partners-pose-the-greatest-security-threat-report.html>.

Robison, Jennifer. "Turning Around Employee Turnover." *Gallup Business Journal*. May 8, 2008. <http://businessjournal.gallup.com/content/106912/Turning-Around-Your-Turnover-Problem.aspx#2>.

Rooney, Ben. "Consumer Confidence Plummets." *CNN Money*. February 24, 2009. <http://money.cnn.com/2009/02/24/news/economy/consumer_confidence/>.

Rousseau, Jean Jacques. *The Social Contract or Principles of Political Right* (1762). Translated by G.D.H. Cole. The Constitution Society, 2013. <www.constitution.org/jjr/socon.htm>.

Sapir, Avinoam. "Presenting SCAN—Scientific Content Analysis." LSI Laboratory for Scientific Interrogation, Inc. Accessed July 9, 2013. www.lsiscan.com/.

Schultz, Howard, and Dori Jones Yang. *Pour Your Heart Into It*. New York: Hyperion, 1997.

Seattle Post Intelligencer. "Starbucks Workers Hit by Alleged Crime Ring." April 22, 2005. <http://www.seattlepi.com/local/article/Starbucks-workers-hit-by-alleged-crime-ring-1171545.php>.

Seattle Times. "Scores of Felons Voted Illegally." January 23, 2005. <http://seattletimes.com/html/localnews/2002158407_felons23m.html>.

Security Executive Council. "Collective Knowledge: Business Continuity Program." Version 1. <https://www.securityexecutivecouncil.com/secstore/index.php?main_page = product_info&cPath = 77_66&products_id = 363>.

Shakespeare, William. *The Tempest*. Edited by William Clark and John Glover. *The Works of William Shakespeare* [Cambridge Edition] [9 vols.] Project Gutenberg, 2007.

Shermer, Michael. "The Soul of Science." *American Scientist*, *93*(no. 2). 2005., 101. Available from http://dx.doi.org/10.1511/2005.2.101.

Shine, Conor. "Consumer Confidence in Food Safety Drops." *Minnesota Daily*. March 1, 2009. <www.mndaily.com/2009/03/01/consumer-confidence-food-safety-drops>.

Society for Human Resource Management (SHRM). "2012 Employee Job Satisfaction and Engagement: How Employees Are Dealing with Uncertainty." October, 2012. <http://www.shrm.org/research/surveyfindings/articles/pages/2012employeejobsatisfaction.aspx>.

Standard and Poor's Rating Services. "Enterprise Risk Management." Accessed July 16, 2013. <www.standardandpoors.com/ratings/erm/en/us/>.

Starbucks Corporation. "Our Starbucks Mission Statement." Accessed July 8, 2013. <http://www.starbucks.com/about-us/company-information/mission-statement>.

___. "Responsibility." Accessed July 11, 2013. <http://www.starbucks.com/responsibility>.

___. "Standards of Business Conduct." Accessed July 11, 2013. <http://www.starbucks.com/assets/eecd184d6d2141d58966319744393d1f.pdf>.

Teaching and Learning Research Programme (TLRP). "Vicarious Learning and Case-Based Teaching of Clinical Reasoning Skills (2004 – 2006)." Accessed July 11, 2013. <www.tlrp.org/proj/phase111/cox.htm>.

The American Red Cross. "Tsunami Recovery Program: Five-Year Report." 2009. <http://www.redcross.org/images/MEDIA_CustomProductCatalog/m3140120_TsunamiRP5yearReport.pdf>.

The ISO 27000 Directory. "An Introduction to ISO 27001, ISO 27002...ISO 27008." Accessed July 23, 2013. <www.27000.org/index.htm>.

The Weather Channel. "Katrina's Statistics Tell Story of Its Wrath." August 21, 2009. <http://www.weather.com/newscenter/topstories/060829katrinastats.html>.

TNS Opinion & Social. "Special Eurobarometer 354: 'Food-Related Risks.'" November, 2010. <http://www.efsa.europa.eu/en/factsheet/docs/reporten.pdf>.

Todd, Deborah "Workzone: Inquiries on Rise amid Resume Fraud." *Pittsburgh Post-Gazette*. August 12, 2012. <http://www.post-gazette.com/stories/business/dateline/workzone-inquiries-on-rise-amid-resume-fraud-648694/>.

United Nations Entity for Gender Equality and the Empowerment of Women. "Fast facts: Statistics on violence against women and girls." Accessed August 20, 2013. <http://www.end-vawnow.org/en/articles/299-fast-facts-statistics-on-violence-against-women-and-girls-.html>.

United States Attorney's Office, Western District of Washington. "Prosecution Priorities for ID Theft Working Group." September 27, 2006. <http://www.justice.gov/usao/waw/press/2006/sep/idtheftworkinggp.html>.

United States Bureau of Labor Statistics. "National Census of Fatal Occupational Injuries in 2011 (Preliminary Results)." US Bureau of Labor Statistics press release, September 20, 2012. US Bureau of Labor Statistics. <http://www.bls.gov/news.release/pdf/cfoi.pdf>.

___(2006). "Survey of Workplace Violence Prevention 2005." October 2006. <www.bls.gov/iif/oshwc/osch0033.pdf>.

United States Customs and Border Protection. "Securing the Global Supply Chain: Customs-Trade Partnership against Terrorism (C-TPAT) Strategic Plan." November 2004. <http://www.cbp.gov/linkhandler/cgov/trade/cargo_security/ctpat/ctpat_program_information/what_is_ctpat/ctpat_strat_plan.ctt/ctpat_strat_plan.pdf>.

United States Department of Homeland Security (DHS). *2009 National Infrastructure Protection Plan: Partnering to Enhance Protection and Resiliency*. Accessed July 8, 2013. <http://www.dhs.gov/national-infrastructure-protection-plan>.

United States Sentencing Commission (USSC). "Guidelines manual." November 1, 2012. <http://www.ussc.gov/Guidelines/index.cfm>.

Von Feldt, Rick. "Nature's Ugly Hand: What We Saw." *Phuket Tsunami Blog*. January 1, 2005. <phukettsunami.blogspot.com/2005/01/natures-ugly-hand-what-we-saw.html>.

Wailgum, Tom. "Metrics for Corporate and Physical Security Programs." *CSO Magazine*. February 1, 2005. www.csoonline.com/article/220023/Metrics_for_Corporate_and_Physical_Security_Programs.

Walshe, Kieran, Gill Harvey, and Pauline Jas. *Connecting Knowledge and Performance in Public Services: From Knowing to Doing*. Cambridge, England: Cambridge University Press, 2010.

Webley, Simon, and Elise More. *Does Business Ethics Pay? Ethics and Financial Performance*. London: Institute of Business Ethics, 2003. <http://www.ibe.org.uk/index.asp?upid = 121& msid = 8#DBEP>.

Westerby, Gerald. *In Hostile Territory*. New York: Harper Business, 1998.

Willox, Norman A., and Thomas M. Regan. "Identity Fraud: Providing a Solution." *Journal of Economic Crime Management*, *1*(no. 1). 2002., 8 <http://www.lcs.syr.edu/faculty/chin/cse774/readings/crime/identity%20theft.pdf>.

Zeller, Tom. "The Nation; The Tao of Enron: Well, It Sounded Good." *The New York Times*. February 24, 2002. <http://www.nytimes.com/2002/02/24/weekinreview/the-nation-the-tao-of-enron-well-it-sounded-good.html>.

INDEX